A Time to Heal

Tarot for the Healing Heart has a simple premise—now is the time to begin healing and resolution. To heal is to make whole. Illness is a message to redirect our lives. Dis-ease (being out of ease) can manifest as physical or emotional pain, broken relationships, or spiritual unrest.

The message of dis-ease is one of hope. The possibilities of the future exist now—not as fantasies, but through the exercise of free choice in the present. Through choice, the future grows as the fruits of our present healing actions.

In Part One of *Tarot for the Healing Heart,* you will learn how to create a healing atmosphere, including creating sacred space, centering, and dream work. In Part Two, explore the meaning of illness and learn to understand your own personal patterns of dis-ease and healing, including letting go of fear.

Health attracts health, and Part Three examines healing as a lifestyle. This section includes healing meditations and visualizations designed to awaken your inner healer, as well as methods of pain reduction.

Part Four explores how to use the entire tarot deck for the express purpose of healing. In-depth descriptions of each card include the card's life lesson and life wisdom.

You do not need to be a tarot expert or a healing practitioner to benefit from this book. All you need is a desire to heal, an open mind, and a courageous heart.

About the Author

Christine Jette (pronounced "Jetty") is a registered nurse and holds a Bachelor of Arts degree in psychology. She is a therapeutic touch practitioner and professional tarot consultant. Christine specializes in health readings combined with hands-on (energetic) healing. She teaches professional writing part-time (non-credit) at the University of Cincinnati. She lives in Cincinnati with her husband and three (spoiled) cats.

TAROT
for the
HEALING HEART

USING INNER WISDOM
TO HEAL BODY AND MIND

CHRISTINE JETTE

Llewellyn Publications
Woodbury, Minnesota

First Edition

Author's photo by Sandy Underwood
Book design and editing by Connie Hill
Cover design by Lisa Novak
Cover photo © 2001 by Doug Deutscher

Library of Congress Cataloging-in-Publication Data
Jette, Christine, 1953–
    Tarot for the healing heart : using inner wisdom to heal body and mind / Christine Jette.
        p. cm.
    Includes bibliographical references and index.
    ISBN 0-7387-0043-6
        1. Tarot. 2. Healing—Miscellanea. I. Title
    BF1879.T2 J475   2001
    133.3'2424—dc21   2001029283

Llewellyn Worldwide does not participate in, endorse, or have any authority or responsibility concerning private business transactions between our authors and the public.
    All mail addressed to the author is forwarded but the publisher cannot, unless specifically instructed by the author, give out an address or phone number.
    Any Internet references contained in this work are current at publication time, but the publisher cannot guarantee that a specific location will continue to be maintained. Please refer to the publisher's website for links to authors' websites and other sources.

Llewellyn Publications
A Division of Llewellyn Worldwide, Ltd.
2143 Wooddale Drive
Woodbury, MN 55125-2989

www.llewellyn.com

 Printed in the United States of America on recycled paper

For Kathleen

Other Books by Christine Jette

Tarot Shadow Work: Using the Dark Symbols to Heal

Forthcoming Books by Christine Jette

Tarot for All Seasons
New Age Writing for Publication

Contents

PART ONE
WHAT EVERYBODY KNOWS

PART FOUR
LION HEART

horsemen of dis-ease. Conscious mind—unconscious body. Life wisdom: listening to the message of dis-ease. The heart of dis-ease: listening to the message in tarot. Letting go of fear: a meditation with the Death card. Good grief. The good grief spread.

PART THREE
HEART AND SOUL

Health attracts health. The inner journey of healing: paying attention to intuition. Healing as a lifestyle. Meditation for the inner healing journey. The open heart: understanding healing. The healer within. Temperance: the healing angel. Contacting the healer within. The cycle of healing: whatever goes around comes around. Outcomes of healing. Why?

Different strokes for different folks. Activities that support the healing process. Psychic play/sacred play. Doing what comes naturally. Perchance to dream: keeping a dream journal. Psychic development and playing with the tarot. It's all in the cards. Your own wise counsel: a meditation with the King or Queen of Cups. Choices, choices. Physician/Healer. Know when to say when. Breaking the pain cycle. Going within to stop pain: a meditation with The Hermit. The compulsion to repeat. The heart of healing. Déjà vu: contemplating the cards. Working your way through.

PART FOUR
WHOLE NEW WORLD

The wounded healer. Tarot and . . . The pendulum swings. Hope and healing for the new millennium.

A gentle reminder. The dance of life. The Major Arcana. The Minor Arcana. Court Cards

Activities

Tarot Spreads

Acknowledgments

Everyone knows there are three rules to good writing.
Unfortunately, no one knows what they are.

W. Somerset Maugham

Writing *Tarot for the Healing Heart* was a challenge. I have the reams of crumpled paper in my wastebasket to prove it. Through all my creative musings—coherent and otherwise—I have been blessed with the stabilizing force of supportive people around me. I send loving energy to the people who support my healing process: Kate, Kathleen, and Mary. Thanks especially to my husband and best friend Tim—his honesty keeps me humble.

I am grateful to be a part of the Llewellyn family of authors. Everyone at Llewellyn is caring and professional—a rare combination of qualities in this high-tech age of impersonal communication. Thank you, Barbara Wright, for believing in my work. Lisa Novak, your cover design is stunning once again. My editor Connie Hill is a quiet presence. Her touch makes my book the best that it can be. Thank you!

The Kingdom of the Sick

Everyone who is born holds a dual citizenship,
in the kingdom of the well and in the kingdom of the sick.

Susan Sontag

I have been a registered nurse (R.N.) since 1977. Through the years, I became despondent over the fragmentation of health care. More and more I saw myself as a skilled mechanic of body parts taking care of the "gallbladder in room 222." Medical specialties further emphasized the remedy-oriented fixing of body segments. Have a problem with the kidneys? Call renal. Heart irregular? Bring in cardiology. Suspect depression? Consult psychiatry. As a charge nurse, I became the division of labor gatekeeper in the kingdom of the sick.

I was encouraged by my supervisors to give sedatives for sleep, instead of backrubs, because it took less time. Nursing stripped itself of its healing heart in the name of technology. As treatments and communications became more complicated, less time was spent at the bedside. I had a hard time fitting love, spirituality, and mystery into my skilled, hectic practice.

I was taught that curing, or absence of symptoms, was my goal and anything less was failure. My job was to save lives, or, at least, postpone death. With this definition of healing, I was doomed to fail because eventually we all die of something. The hospitals where I worked were filled with profoundly ill people. They were poked, prodded, and chemically treated. The war against death raged.

Tarot for the Healing Heart is a labor of love—born out of my frustration with modern health care, my own experience with chronic illness and the mystery of healing. It explores the messages of dis-ease (being out of ease), and looks at ways to use the messages for growth. Let an intuitive guiding force lead you to your correct path of healing. As you soar to a higher overview, may your life be filled with health and happiness.

PART ONE

WHAT EVERYBODY KNOWS

A new idea is first condemned as ridiculous,
then dismissed as trivial, until finally,
it becomes what everybody knows.

William James

Chapter 1

THE TIME TO HEAL

Take the time to come home to yourself everyday.

Robin Casarjean

Linking to a timeless rite: holistic healing, tarot, and you

TIME Magazine estimates that Americans spend $30 billion each year on alternative health practices. With the start of the new millennium, attitudes toward health and healing are changing. People are beginning to take an active role in their own well being. Many are trying Yoga, Tai Chi, meditation, herbal remedies, and natural medicines. Some hospitals are now offering massage, healing touch, reflexology, aromatherapy, chakra balancing, Reiki, acupressure, and hypnosis.

Modern medical science excels at repairing broken bones and organs, inventing prostheses, and using diagnostic technology. It successfully doses conditions such as high blood pressure and diabetes. Perhaps its greatest contributions are preventing childhood illnesses such as polio and eliminating contagion—small pox is an example.

Medical science falls short in treating chronic stress-related illnesses: migraine headaches, fibromyalgia, irritable bowel, gastric ulcer, insomnia, chronic fatigue syndrome, depression, anxiety, panic attacks, and seasonal affective disorder (SAD).

Yet these conditions respond well to "alternative" types of therapy such as meditation, acupressure, reflexology, massage, biofeedback, aromatherapy, herbal remedies, and healing touch. "Alternative" treatments focus on the mind-body connection, as both a cause *and* a cure of illness. The emphasis is placed on the total well-being of the person—body, emotions, mind, and spirit are inseparable and interdependent.

Good health depends on many factors: emotions, psychological makeup, heredity, health habits, lifestyle, financial support, social support, and diet as fuel for the physical body. Each plays an important part in our ability to live well—what affects one affects all.

Healing is an ancient tradition based on the feminine, spiritual qualities of empathy, nurturance, and intuition. The most sacred tool we have for healing is the intuitive ability to listen to the still small voice within that tells us what health and happiness mean to us. When you use tarot for healing you are linked to a timeless rite. Wellness is mind, body, and spirit in balance. Tarot reveals areas that are out of balance and gives advice on the best ways to restore order.

Healing heart tarot offers a way to step outside ordinary consciousness and discover a connection between you, the healer within, and a universal healing force. The cards' images are filled with healing energies that direct you toward wholeness, and this book guides you step-by-step through the process. Holistic healing, including the use of tarot for healing, is more than a vague philosophy—it's a way of being fully alive every single day.

Tarot for the Healing Heart shows you that powerful healing does not emerge from laboratories and technological advances. Instead, it is the use of self, in a loving and compassionate way, which provides you with your most powerful tool for healing. Healing is a timeless rite, and health and happiness are "in the cards" for you.

The time to heal

Illness is a puzzle. Many pieces fit together to give a complete picture. Healing is not an all-or-nothing proposition. There is no one "right" way to heal and no two healing experiences are the same. The amount of time you spend with the activities in this book depends upon your personal goals for healing. Be as elaborate or simple as your intuition tells you to be.

Activities include ten original tarot layouts for healing; tarot card meditations for releasing the healer within; exploring healing as a lifestyle; keeping a healing journal; creating an atmosphere for healing; breaking the pain cycle; and developing psychic ability through sacred play with tarot cards. "When Spider Webs Unite" focuses on using the energy of tarot to form your own circle of support. The time you invest in any of these is your choice.

Tarot for the Healing Heart helps you find solutions to life's challenges. Every tarot card has actions to support the healing process—practical hands-on suggestions to activate the healing energies of that card. Journal questions spark inner wisdom (see chapter 2). No prior knowledge of tarot is required.

A word about chronic pain

"I'm sorry, there's nothing more we can do for you." If you suffer from long-term pain and have heard this line before, please don't give up. Keep searching. It's not that you have intractable pain—it's that you haven't found a way to relieve it yet.

With long-term pain, however, it is important to note that relief can best be measured in increments. For example, if you rate your pain on a scale of one to ten, with ten being the worst, you may first notice a comfort shift from nine to seven. With regular use, the methods of pain reduction described in this book (such as centering and meditation) will offer you *gradual* improvement over several weeks.

Getting the most from Tarot for the Healing Heart

Healing is a process. Take your time. Each chapter builds upon itself and is best understood if taken in order. This is not a basic tarot text, but rather, a way to use the cards for healing.

If you want more information on traditional tarot, visit a bookstore and let your inner wisdom guide you. Many wonderful books are available on the subject. Use any deck that appeals to you. The healing heart tarot layouts found throughout this book may be photocopied for repeated use over time.

In chapter 2, "Clearing a Path," important preliminary steps are covered to create a healing atmosphere. These include creating sacred space, centeredness, affirming the intention to heal, meditation, keeping a journal, and dream work.

Chapter 3, "The Broken Heart," gives an overview of illness and provides you with tools for understanding your personal patterns of dis-ease. A meditation called "Choosing Your Karma" focuses on finding your personal power.

The defects and flaws that keep us from health are not personal failures, but wounds. Chapter 4, "The Heart of Dis-ease," examines the choices you are making, not as defects, but as wounds exposed. Here you will find your personal meaning of dis-ease, or life lesson, and explore things that go bump in the night.

By listening to the message of dis-ease from your body, you start to hear your own life wisdom and create a healing cycle. Emphasis is placed on the fact that physical handicap and permanent injuries do not interfere with our ability to give and receive love. By understanding your body's messages, you begin to learn life wisdom.

Health attracts health. Chapter 5, "The Open Heart," begins by looking at the important role of healing as a lifestyle. You gain awareness through an activity called "The Inner Healing Journey." Finally, you awaken the healer within; a meditation with Temperance, the healing angel, offers a visualization for self-healing.

Chapter 6, "The Heart of Healing," looks at activities that support the healing process. Methods of pain reduction are explored in a meditation with The Hermit called "Going Within to Stop Pain." You will learn to hear your own wise counsel through activities with the King and Queen of Cups. Practical suggestions give you ideas on how to find continued support for the healing process.

Because we want to help others, there is a tendency to become healers before we ourselves are healed. Chapter 7, "Horizons," explores using *Tarot for the Healing Heart* to heal others, and concludes with a prediction for the new millennium.

Chapter 8, "Healing Heart Tarot," explains how to use an entire tarot deck for the express purpose of healing. It begins with important preliminary steps to take when working with the cards.

You are the healer/doctor

Think back to a moment in your childhood when you knew that magic was real: it could have been looking at a butterfly, serving tea to all your imaginary friends, or being barefoot on lush, green grass. Remember that wonderful time when you knew God, Goddess, Spirit, or Source existed (whatever this personally means to you), and being alive was a natural, holy experience. So natural, in fact, you didn't give Mother/Father God a second thought. You just floated into the peaceful, loving arms of a creator/creatrix.

As a child, you probably let yourself go into whatever task was at hand. You naturally, without conscious thought, put your full energy into your activities, whether it was making mud pies, helping your mother set the table, or keeping score at a Red Sox game. You didn't think about being playful or creative—you just were.

Now think to a time in adulthood when you felt that same sense of magic: being given over to the life energy that flows out of you from an internal source. Maybe it was at the birth of your child, the first time you fell in love, or in completing a creative project. Do you remember the abandon you felt? The colors were brighter, the air more fragrant, the tastes sweeter, and all was right with the world?

Perhaps your best ideas come to you when you least expect them. You're taking a shower, looking at a cat, or watching the sunset and, suddenly, you have a wonderful idea. It has emerged from deep within you. Perhaps you have struggled with a solution to a problem and, after a good night's sleep, the answer appeared from nowhere.

All this—a sense of magic and wonder, good ideas, hunches, intuition, and solutions to unsolvable problems—comes from a deep source of inner knowing central to your being. It is your divine inner spark and I call it the healer within. It comes from an awareness of our common source.

All of us can learn to tap into this deep source within us. We have experienced the healer within at random moments all our lives, whether we recognized it or not. A good example is the ability to perform incredible acts of strength during moments of crisis, such as lifting a car off a loved one after an accident. Another is the mother who awakens moments before the smoke detector goes off and is able to rescue her family from a fiery death because of it. The creative force is always with us and available to us. It takes practice to become fully aware of it—and even more practice to release the creative, healing energies at will.

The healing process is more involved with getting obstacles out of the way rather than pulling up creative energy. The activities in *Tarot for the Healing Heart* are designed to remove blocks. Once the blocks are gone, creative, healing energy flows up from inside us like a bubbling spring. Much of illness is a result of blocking our creative energies. The process of healing is the process of dissolving blocks and releasing our creative force for health.

Another way to look at healing is as a process of letting go, surrendering, fully feeling and releasing pain, fear, and blockages. If we are willing to feel the depth of our emotions for even a moment, we will release the block, much like the release of air in a blown-up balloon with a pin.

It can be frightening to believe we are able to heal ourselves by listening to our spiritual, creative inner voice. We begin to hope, and we begin to fear that hope, because healing carries with it the responsibility of personal choice. When we choose to behave differently, we change, and it is the change that causes fear. For most of us, learning to trust the inner voice is the most difficult aspect of healing.

The real key to healing and change is to feel all our feelings, surrender, let go, and to relax. It is in this state of relaxation that the healer within can emerge. *You* are the healer, the doctor. All healing comes from within. Absolutely everyone can learn to contact and direct the healer within because we all carry the divine spark—but it takes honest intent and practice to contact and direct the healer within at will.

Mystical energy is limitless and connecting to the endless supply of spiritual energy through the use of the tarot cards is the focus of this book. Using nothing but your personal energy for healing is draining and less powerful. For now, accept the fact that a common well of unending healing energy is available to you—and always has been.

A word to the wise

Tarot for the Healing Heart complements, but does not replace, standard medical care. Changes come from within an individual and the activities here are accessories to healing. Tarot work supplements professional care, bringing the unconscious mind into harmony with the physical self to assist the healing process.

Treatment is your choice. *Tarot for the Healing Heart* can help you understand the reasons behind dis-ease, but it does not diagnose, treat, or prescribe; and it is not intended for primary medical intervention. If you have symptoms, contact your health professional of choice before proceeding with any activity in this book.

Chapter 2

Clearing a Path: The Tools of Healing

Affirmations are like prescriptions for certain
aspects of yourself you want to change.

Jerry Frankhauser

Sacred space

Healing is a complex process generating many levels of psychic activity. It is important to be centered and protected during healing work. To serve this purpose, you can create a sanctuary, a safe haven to honor your healing quest. It needs to be a quiet place where you will not be interrupted.

Use your own spiritual system when creating sanctuary. Your intuitive, creative self is fed by images. Because of this, you may want to set up an altar in your special place of sanctuary. The altar provides a visual focus for directing healing energy.

Small rituals you create for yourself are good for the soul. Building an altar literally means putting spirituality into physical form. It will connect you with your deepest, innermost self. You will learn to hear the still small voice within that gives you messages about your illness, growth, and healing.

You can put pictures, tarot cards, candles, incense, spiritual symbols, special momentos, crystals, and flowers on your altar. Anything at all—as long as it holds special meaning for you. Use blue accessories for peaceful healing, red or orange to represent vitality, white for pure energy and elements in balance. Green confers regeneration and growth. Purple is effective for serious illness. Red or white carnations radiate healing energy. Compatible incense includes sandalwood, apple, gardenia, cinnamon, cedar, or rose. Your healing journal and tarot card layouts can be kept on the altar. You will probably replace items as your focus changes.

Everything about your sanctuary and altar is personal and will reflect your individuality, your life experiences, your pain, your healing. Anything that brings your spirituality into physical form has a rightful place on the healing altar.

As you sit before your altar in your chosen space, take some time to breathe deeply and do nothing. When you allow yourself to do nothing, new connections and insights will occur because you open up to the possibility of hearing your higher self. The healer within speaks to you in whispers and cannot be heard above the din of everyday living. It demands an inner silence to make itself known.

You may feel a resistance to creating a sanctuary for yourself because the demands and stresses of life impose upon your time. Start with ten or fifteen minutes a day devoted to your healing. Build from there as you experience the benefits of sanctuary. If you cannot find ten minutes in a day to devote to yourself, ask yourself why. Much illness arises out of having no room for ourselves in our own hearts. As women, we take care of everyone but ourselves. Think of sanctuary time as the gift of love and nurturing that you give yourself. You will be amazed at the results.

Healing heart tarot

A physical illness doesn't appear out of empty space. It originates on the spiritual, psychological, or emotional plane first. The higher self communicates to us through symbols, and symptoms symbolically reflect a deeper meaning. Our physical (outer) bodies reflect our deeper (inner) selves. In a real way, illness is the physical language of the psyche. Tarot can provide the key to translating the message.

The universal symbolism of tarot can illuminate all aspects of your life—physical, emotional, psychological, and spiritual. The cards are a reflection of you through all levels of being. The goal of working with tarot for healing is to bring body, mind, and spirit into balance to support the healing process. (Please see "A word to the wise" at the end of chapter 1, p. 9.)

Working with tarot stimulates the intuitive, creative part of the brain. We learn to use our imagination to make connections between physical, emotional, psychological, and spiritual conditions. Since physical symptoms are symbolic, we stop taking them at face value and listen for the message. What are the symptoms trying to tell us about our direction?

Tarot provides a way to relate everyday life to a larger picture. The images present an opportunity to examine our lives against an eternal backdrop. We begin to understand a higher order of things, and awareness of something larger than ourselves is the essence of healing. Refer to chapter 8 for a detailed description of working with tarot for the healing heart.

Tarot is a reflection of you

Tarot is a mirror extension of yourself because your life is a reflection of your beliefs. Interpretation is in the eye of the beholder. Because of this, *Tarot for the Healing Heart* does not ascribe to one type of deck. Work with any deck that appeals to you.

Every tarot card conveys information through its activity, color, scene, the people, or the attitude. Tarot symbols affect our perceptions and activate our inner selves. The art of tarot shows forces and circumstances that have been active in our lives at one time or another.

Approach tarot as the picture book version of your life story. The "art" of a tarot reading lies within the symbols of the cards. The best tarot work comes from the heart, not the intellect. Your heart responds to the pictures. You "read" a card by comparing the images to events in your own life. Does a card remind you of a situation, event, relationship, or method of communicating? You can learn many things about yourself by attending to the symbolism of tarot on a regular basis. Approach tarot with heart and your mind will follow.

The key to understanding tarot is to allow it to come to life. The sooner you connect a card with a real situation, the sooner you become a skilled interpreter. For example, if you are feeling depressed and the Four of Cups appears in a reading, look at the picture on the card and feel the depression. When you see it again in another layout, you will remember the feeling and know its meaning without memorizing anything. Always look at the card with which you are working. No amount of memorization can replace the artistic symbolism of the picture. Connecting to a picture is the fastest way to learn tarot, no matter which deck you are using.

It is important to get a basic idea of traditional meanings because this will keep you out of fantasy and wishful thinking. It is also important to give your intuitive self some latitude because this keeps you from rigidity. You probably trust your intellect. Learning to respect and trust your intuition is the focus of healing with tarot.

You may find propping a card in front of you while you work with it is helpful. All the exercises in this book are intended for use with your tarot deck in sight. You will benefit from the activities faster if you know the pictures of your own deck better than my words. Don't rely on your intellect and good memory. Your intuitive self reads the cards and is in love with the artwork. As you use the cards more, you will learn to trust your inner wisdom.

Now to the burning question: Can you really read for yourself? Of course. Be aware of the potential for wishful thinking. Because your own concerns may interfere, the fortunetelling aspect of tarot may not be reliable, but you can read for yourself in a different way—for healing and growth.

If you are too emotionally involved with an issue, do a reading for yourself and then compare the reading with one done for you. Talk it over with a trusted friend or adviser to get a "reality check." Reading for yourself can be a rich source of the insight needed to initiate and support the healing process.

Ritual and tarot: deciding what you value

It is confusing to pick up six different tarot books and read six different ways to handle and store the cards. You can drive yourself crazy trying to do everything you read in a book. The purpose of a ritual is to help you focus on the task at hand. So how do you decide whether or not to clear the cards with moonlight, face north while working with them, shuffle to the right, burn clary sage, or store the cards in a pine box? Opinions vary on what to do with tarot decks.

Rituals are a personal matter. If you like rituals and they help you concentrate on working with the cards, use them. No ritual you do is sacred unless it is sacred to you. If you develop a habit because it centers your attention or signals your intuition, then it has value. The most powerful rituals are the ones you invent. Never do something because a book tells you to do it. Listen to and trust your inner wisdom. Be aware of why you do what you do. Use whatever ritual feels right when working with the cards, or not.

You will not, at any time, be told how to shuffle, deal, clean, or store your deck. It's your choice. Treat the cards the way you treat anything else of value. Tarot can be a powerful tool for healing and growth, but the magic does not come from the cards: the magic comes from you.

Meditation and tarot

Meditation allows you to quiet your mind and access your inner wisdom. It can also strengthen your spiritual connection. The greatest aid to meditation is your intention to still the mind. The easiest way to do this is to concentrate on slow, deep breathing until you feel yourself relax. If your mind wanders, simply bring it back to your slow, deep breathing.

If you are skilled at seeing pictures in your mind's eye, imagine a beautiful nature scene. It can be a forest, beach, or anywhere at all that you find restful. Imagery such as this can take you to a peaceful place where you are calm and the mind gradually becomes still. Chanting and sounds made on instruments such as drums or bells can be powerful focal points for meditation. So can your tarot cards.

Try this: Select any tarot card you like. Prop it in front of you so you can see it without straining your eyes. Take slow, deep breaths until you feel yourself relax. Breathe out worries and pain; breathe in a feeling of well-being. When you are relaxed, look at your chosen tarot card. Concentrate on breathing in a slow, deep way. Attend to whatever thoughts come into your mind as you gaze at the picture.

Mentally converse with the card. Ask it about its healing potential. Let your thoughts flow. If your critical censor shouts at you about the silliness of talking to a tarot card, tell it to be quiet and bring your attention back to deep breathing. Stay with the card for awhile and your inner wisdom will whisper to you.

Strong feelings toward a card—both positive and negative—are usually a signal that the card holds an important message for you. The healing messages of tarot will be explored in depth throughout the remainder of this book.

The energy to heal

Modern medicine's approach to illness does not acknowledge energy in and around the human body. This energy, or universal life force, has many names: *prana* in Hinduism, *chi* in China, *ki* in Japan, *mana* by the Huna of Hawaii. Most recently, it has been called "bioenergy."[1]

When a healer puts her or his hands on a person who is ill, both healer and patient become warm. Energy-based healing is grounded in ancient tradition. When you use tarot cards in health and illness readings, you are accessing this ancient universal life force—or energy. Please refer to chapter 8 for ways to use the entire tarot deck in health and illness readings.

Your healing journal

Keeping a journal allows you to put into words your innermost thoughts without fear of criticism. A journal is your personal property and can be kept confidential, much like a diary. Many beautiful blank books are available, but you need not spend a lot of money on your journal. A three-ring notebook is adequate. You can add entries on loose-leaf paper. Perhaps you'll want to decorate the outside of your notebook. Creativity unlocks intuition—make the journal a unique expression of you.

The healing effect from journaling comes from the process of writing your thoughts, feelings, insights, and observances. You can be sad, silly, angry, profane, or anything else you want to be without fear of reprisal. The journal becomes the chronicle of your healing process. Whether you share it with anyone is up to you. As you reread entries, you will find the journal to be a record of growth, wisdom, and healing.

Journal entries can be jotted down at odd moments, but you may want to establish a regular time for writing about the healing process. Date each entry. The activities suggested in this book can become part of your journal. Once the value of journal keeping has been established, you will find it becomes a trusted friend—a daily ritual during which you record your feelings, traumas, pain, joy, triumphs, and insights.

Record and date every tarot activity and keep it in your journal. Each tarot reading is one step in your journey toward healing. Keeping a record over time allows you to monitor your inner development. Always date your tarot entries.

If you notice some of the cards repeating themselves in your heart layouts, there is a message calling for your attention. A theme in your life, represented by the repetitive cards, needs examination. Sometimes the messages of dis-ease are not immediately clear. By keeping a tarot journal, you can review confusing readings next week or next month. You may be surprised at how much sense the cards make at a later date.

Honor all information you receive, regardless of whether you grasp it today. Adopt an attitude of respectful regard and do not dismiss cards you don't like or don't understand. The message is in the cards—if you stay with the cards. Over time, with patience and practice, the puzzle pieces will fall into place.

The healing power of dreams

Illness gives us the opportunity to work with the guidance from deep within the unconscious. Dreams at this time can be a source of wisdom and healing. Dreams remind us of what we fear and what we need to accept in order to become whole. The only person who can interpret your dream is you. Expect a dream and the ability to recall it—then prepare to encounter your own deep nature.

Keep an open journal or tape recorder by your bed. Tell yourself, as you drift off to sleep, that you will remember your dreams. Write or record the dream the moment you awaken. Write the sequence in the present tense, as though it were happening now (i.e., "I am walking on a beach," not "I was walking"). This keeps the dream alive. Give it a name based on the content, such as "The Beach" or "Deserted Highway."

Allow the dream to work on you during the day, especially during quiet time or meditation. Be willing to suspend disbelief and let the images come alive without overanalyzing them. Dream interpretation is a cautious balance between logic and intuition. If you get it wrong the first time, your unconscious will try again. By approaching dream work with expectation, honesty, and care, your dreams will become a deep well of wisdom that supports the healing process.

Centering: the art of knowing yourself

How can we heal ourselves if we do not know ourselves? And how can we know ourselves if we are unable (or unwilling) to sit with ourselves—warts and all? We can't. When we become human "doings," our attempts to run away from ourselves only lead to more stress.

Centering (breathing, meditation, and stillness) is the art of knowing yourself from the inside out. It provides a solution to the relentless intensity of daily life and a way to meet the challenges of taking care of you—for a change.

Think of centering as standing on solid ground inside yourself. Illness and healing involve every aspect of your life on four levels—physical, emotional, psychological, and spiritual. It takes a lot of energy to be sick and a lot more energy to heal. Centering prepares you to work effectively with all four levels of dis-ease and wellness by quieting the mind, relaxing the body, and settling the emotions. When mind, body, and emotions are ready, healing occurs through the action of spirit.

Centering is an act of self-searching, a going within to explore the deepest meanings of your existence. It is a journey to understand your own being and your relationship with the universe. In the stillness, you can ask questions. If you listen, you will hear profound answers. These insights come from the inner self, teacher, or guide who is a reflection of your personal power. By withdrawing your attention from the outer world, you will form an inner intention to heal yourself (more on the intention to heal in the next section).

To center yourself, start simply. Begin by practicing in your quiet place of sanctuary. Eventually you will be able to center at any time, in any situation. Inhale and exhale slowly. Become aware of the space between breaths. Notice the feeling of quiet, almost as if time is suspended. If your attention wanders, bring it back to your slow, deep breathing.

Once you experience the stillness, if only for a minute or so, you are ready to go deeper. Sit comfortably. Loosen any tight clothing. Close your eyes and become aware of your breathing. Focus your attention in the area of your heart and think of something that symbolizes peace to you—the ocean, an animal, a meadow or tree. Feel the peace of the image as you breathe deeply and focus on the heart area. Think of the peaceful feeling as coming from inside yourself. Say out loud, "I am calm and centered. I am at peace."

Stay with the peaceful feeling. Allow it to travel to all parts of your body. To take it one step further, try to identify or focus on the part of your consciousness that senses energy and creates visualizations, for it is here that your higher self resides. Keep your healing journal nearby to jot down key thoughts and symbols because your healer within speaks to you in images during these times of quiet solitude.

To bring yourself back to ordinary consciousness, move your feet and place your hands on the chair or floor. Say, "I am grounded and fully awake. I am at peace and rested." You may feel lightheaded, so continue to take deep breaths and wait until you are aware of the surroundings before standing up.

Affirmation: the intention to heal

The use of conscious intent is essential in healing. By becoming aware of yourself, you will be able to work on and heal yourself. When we develop a sensitivity to our motivations behind the desire to heal, we learn about the intention to heal. Silence, solitude, reflection, and thought are the important elements required for cultivating this sensitivity. Once the reflective process begins, introspection leads to a spiritual journey of healing.

When we have the intention to heal without a hidden agenda, we can detach from the outcome of treatment. Although we want to improve, by having the intention to heal, we can relax and let go of a specific outcome. If we believe healing to be an integration of physical, emotional, mental, and creative energies, resulting in a sense of wholeness, then healing can take place whether or not there is a return to physical function.

We make a clear intent to help ourselves, let go of the need to control the result, and trust that our healing work will restore order within the body exactly as it is supposed to do. The intention to heal is not emotion or a personal desire, but a much deeper force. We mobilize ourselves, mind and body, to carry out the specific purpose of healing.

One of the best ways to develop a pure intention to heal is by using affirmations on a regular basis. We attract to ourselves what we expect. If we expect illness, we become ill. Likewise, if we expect to heal, healing comes our way. Affirmations, spoken out loud, reprogram the subconscious mind to make the necessary changes of intent.

The secret for successful use of affirmation is to delete all negative wording. For example, instead of saying, "I am no longer ill," proclaim "I am healing," Don't write "I have no pain," because this puts the idea of pain in your subconscious; write "I feel well."

Affirmations can be written, spoken, read, or heard on a tape recorder, according to the sense that works best for you. Set aside a specific time of day and write, speak, or listen to the affirmation. The more you use the affirmation, the sooner the reprogramming will take place. Write the affirmation and put it in a place you will see everyday, such as on your bathroom mirror or refrigerator.

You will need to practice the affirmation at least two weeks before you begin to notice any real difference. Given time, affirmations can and do dramatically change your life. Phrases you create for yourself are better than using the words of others. Keep the affirmation in the present tense (I am . . .) and positive ("I am well," rather than "I am no longer sick").

To get you started, try the affirmation below. Once you find your own voice, use your words, not mine. Write your personal affirmation of healing on the first page of your journal. Repeat it every day.

Say aloud: "I am calm, strong, and centered. I am at peace, safe, and secure. I enjoy who I am. I expect healing and I am thankful for it." Know that your healing has begun.

Affirmation: the circle of protection

Sometimes we are the targets for other people's anxiety, anger, fear, negative thoughts, and emotions. Theses powerful energies can be easily absorbed and, as a consequence, we feel some degree of disturbance. Have you ever experienced headache or fatigue after being in a stadium or shopping mall? We can be in situations such as meetings or crowds where these negative energies are moving about and absorb them without realizing what is happening to us.

The negative energy usually enters our bodies through the solar plexus, an area around the navel, but it can enter any place we allow it to enter. An easy way to protect yourself from draining energy is to imagine a circle of intense white or purple light surrounding your entire body, like an orb or sphere. Only positive energy can enter and negativity is deflected because the circle is sealed. The negative energy is not returned to the sender, but is sent out to the universe where it can be recycled. This method of protection is sometimes called shielding. For extra "oomph," visualize a golden disc of light around your solar plexus, or belly area, as soon as you enter an atmosphere of negative thoughts and emotions.

You can also send the energy of blue or white light out to a room, bringing a peaceful atmosphere. Green light offers balance and pink light radiates loving energy to change thoughts and feelings for the better. Simply see the room filling with light and surrounding everyone in it. If you have difficulty seeing something in your mind's eye, actually say to yourself that you are sending this light to the room and the people in it, for the good of all. As with the circle of protection, your intent is all that matters. You do not have to *see* a thing for it to be true. Honestly ask for help—then trust that you will receive it.

The truth is, if we do not need to absorb the pain and illness of others, we will not take on any of their negativity. The clearer we are that people have their own power and the ability to heal themselves by taking full responsibility for their lives, the easier it will be to avoid their negative energy. Their dis-ease need not be our dis-ease, unless we give them permission to enter.

No energy can stick to us without our cooperation, at least on the unconscious level. There is always an aspect of ourselves that invites any energy— good, bad, or indifferent—into us. Addressing the part of us that invites negative energy into our lives is critical to engaging the healing process. As we become healthier, we may discover that shielding is rarely needed because health attracts health—and health is the most powerful energy of all.

Healing guides and helpers

As you work with the tarot exercises in this book and attune yourself to the energy of the healing process, you will become aware of receiving help from a higher frequency vibration than the physical. I call this presence a *healing guide* or *spirit helper*. You can call upon your healing guide to give you the insight and courage needed to heal old wounds.

Your healing guide comes out of love alone and its only motive is to help you.* Ask that the guide who comes to assist you be of white light, aligned with the highest good of all and filled with universal love, truth and wisdom. If you ever find unhelpful spirits in your aura, (rare if you're grounded, centered, and protected), surround yourself with white light and ask your healing guide to escort them on to their next appropriate step for their highest good.

---

*   The English language does not have a personal pronoun meaning "he *or* she." Solving this dilemma is tricky. In my own experience, a healing guide is masculine and feminine, a very balanced, intelligent, complete, and evolved energy. Only you can decide if your personal healing guide is "he, she, s/he, or it." I have found that guides love to impart information. If you are uncertain, and gender is important to you, simply ask your guide.

After your meditations, layouts, or journal entries are completed, thank the spirit guides and healers for their help. Release them from your grasp so that they can go where they are most needed. Despite all doubts, worries, or fears, the healing guides will always come when called upon.

You may want to ask your healing guide to direct a healing through your hand chakras, the energy centers located in both palms. If you are uncomfortable with the idea, simply skip the exercise. Never do something from this (or any) book just because it's there. Understand your own motivations and know why you choose to do something—or not. If you choose to move on, make an entry in your journal about sources of help available to you according to your own spiritual belief system—and your willingness to ask for that assistance.

To begin the exercise, sit down before your healing altar, center yourself, cast a circle of protection and state an affirmation of healing as described earlier. Say something like this:*

> I call upon my healing guide(s) to assist me with my healing. I ask that only the most perfect, powerful, correct, and harmonious energies be with me and that they be compatible with my purposes of healing. I ask that my guides be in the most understandable form possible, its equivalent or better. May my healing be for the good of all, harming no one, according to free will, so must it be.

Open your hand chakras, the energy centers in both palms, by bringing light above you through your head, shoulders, and arms. Have the light come to rest in the palms of both hands and visualize the centers of each palm opening. Briskly rub the palms of your hands together for several seconds to increase the energy flow. Ask your guide to enter your hand chakras in a way that lets you actually *feel* the energy.

Allow your healing master to guide your hands around and over your body and aura. Or, you can simply invite the guide into your aura, the energy field around your body, and let it work on you. Sit back and enjoy the process. Healing guides love to help. If you like, ask your guide to do a healing on you every day, especially as you work your way through *Tarot for the Healing Heart*.

---

* Note: Your own words always work best.

At the end of the healing session, when you feel a change in the energy flow, say to yourself, in your own words, "This healing is over and I am thankful for it." Thank the guide(s) directly and make your separations by asking them to move back behind you, outside of your aura. Say: "I bring all of my energy, and only my energy, back into my body. Stay if you will. If you must leave, go in peace, back to your native habitat, and harm no one along the way." Breathe deeply and place both hands, palms down, on the chair to ground energy. Slowly get up, stretch, and move your body. Gently shake both hands and wash them with soap and water. Make an entry in your journal about the healing guide experience.

Sometimes, the hardest part of healing isn't getting started; it's knowing when to stop. Most of the time, you'll know because the energy will just stop—there will be a cessation of energy flow through your hands. There may be times, however, when you're not sure. You can test it by slowly moving your hands away from your body. If the energy is still present, you will feel a subtle pull or pulse. Accept the fact that it may be difficult to tell while you are still learning about your guide and the flow of healing energy. The best suggestion is to simply end the healing when it feels right to do so. Trust your intuition.

I encourage you to bring your guide in to do healings on yourself, especially after a tarot exercise. Guides enjoy it—it's play to them. Relax and work in a calm manner, letting go of preconceived notions. Allow your awareness of healing energy to develop naturally over time. I do not include this aspect of healing with your guide to impress or mystify you. I want to demonstrate the depth of love which surrounds you—and always has, even without your awareness of it.

Your healing guide wants to be useful. Ask for her or his presence whenever you do an exercise in this book. Continue to build a relationship over the next several weeks and months. By actively engaging your healing guide in a partnership with you, your relationship will grow stronger and the healing aspect of the tarot cards will make more sense.

Guides have different purposes but they always work for your highest good. They also have their own paths to follow. When you grow and change, your healing guide may change. Ask them to tell you when it's time for them to move on. They can introduce you to your new guide when the time is right. One final note: You may have more than one healing guide, each with a distinct purpose. If this is the case for you, what purpose does each guide have? When in doubt, ask—then trust the answer you receive.

Notes to Chapter 2

1. Campbell, Eileen and J. H. Brennan. *Body, Mind and Spirit: A Dictionary of New Age Ideas, People, Places and Terms.* (Boston, Charles E. Tuttle Company, Inc., 1994), p. 221.

PART TWO

Lion Heart

We teach best what we need to know.

Anonymous

Chapter 3

THE BROKEN HEART: UNDERSTANDING ILLNESS

A broken heart is like a desert wherein
can flourish no green thing.
Washington Irving

Love your body, heal your body

Imagery has been used in healing since the first shamans and priestesses appeared. Healing temples functioned on the premise that visions and dreams contained knowledge about emotional, psychological, physical, and spiritual health. As children, we are natural visual thinkers, aware of the imaginative, symbolic realms, but these abilities are soon suppressed. *Tarot for the Healing Heart* will help you contact deep feelings, sensitivities, and capacities—and in the process, reintegrate the intuitive, imaginative, feminine side of yourself so vital to self-healing. You will learn much about the power of image as opposed to the word. This experience will help you later in the book, as you work with the powerful healing images of tarot.

If we do not love ourselves we cannot heal ourselves. The body is the unique medium through which we experience and express love. Love of self means, in part, love of our bodily experience and expression. Love of our own bodies is a difficult task in this country where the commercial norm of women's bodies is improbable for most, if not impossible.

We must be thin. Rounded abdomens, varicose veins, and wrinkles are downright disgusting. Pictures of women more beautiful than ourselves assault us at every turn. Each year, anorexia nervosa kills young women in pursuit of the perfect body. Loving our own bodies becomes a competitive, deadly sport.

Marlene Dietrich, a movie siren of the 1930s, spent the last years of her life in seclusion because she didn't want the world to see her as an old woman. What a sad statement against womanhood. In order to heal yourself, you must set aside the external images of transient beauty in favor of a lasting experience that occurs within. We cannot heal what we hate. Health, and the resultant beauty, comes from the inside out. The following exercise will help you identify with the beauty of the embodied spirit—and set the atmosphere for healing on all levels.

Mirror, mirror, on the wall

This exercise can be done with or without clothing. Choose a time when you will be undisturbed. If you like, burn incense and light a candle. Stand before a full-length mirror. Begin by breathing slowly and deeply. Exhale all your concerns of the day. Inhale a feeling of calm and well-being. When you are relaxed, focus your attention on the image of yourself in the mirror. State aloud what you like, for example, "I like my eyes." Start at the head and work your way down to the toes. Each time you come to something you like about yourself, stop and say out loud why you like it, "I like my eyes because they are a beautiful color."

Now fix your gaze once again on your head and state aloud what you dislike, such as "I don't like my nose." Continue downward, stopping to recognize what you find unattractive. Be sure to state why you don't like something, "I don't like my nose because it's too big." Why do you feel this way? Does your nose work properly? Can you breathe? Is your sense of smell developed? If so, why don't you like your nose? Did someone tell you once that it was too big? Whose truth is this? Yours or another person's?

Next, focus your attention on the area around the heart. This is the area of your spiritual ideal and it is where all healing takes place. While looking at your body in the mirror, breathe out your cares. Breathe in a beautiful rose-pink light. Let it surround your heart and fill you with a sense of well being. Allow the rose-pink light to expand, fill your body, and radiate all around you. Take your time, breathe slowly. You feel safe, calm, and loved.

Continue focusing your attention on the heart. If your mind wanders, bring it back to your slow, deep breathing. Close your eyes. Send a beam of this beautiful light from your heart to an unliked body part that you identified earlier. Let the light penetrate every pore of this unloved part of you. Feel this area of your body begin to get warm and radiate the beautiful light. Place your hand over the unloved part of you and say, "All this is me and all of me is loved and lovable."

Continue to send universal love (the rose-pink light) to every aspect of your body. Repeat, "All of this is me and all of me is loved and lovable." When you have drenched your entire body in rose light, open your eyes and look at yourself again. What do you see? How do you feel about what you see? Know you have entered sacred space to be with the beauty of the loving, embodied spirit. Be still and at peace with the beauty within you. Allow your thoughts to enter and leave without censure, and make an entry in your healing journal.

Loving our bodies does not mean we lack the desire to improve upon or heal our bodies. Quite the contrary—only through self-love can lasting change occur.

The dance of life

We are either in a state of wholeness (health) or seeking to return to it (illness). Dis-ease (being out of ease) is a condition of energy imbalance or disorder. Healing restores order. In science, the term for this wonderful system of checks and balances is called "homeostasis" and pertains to the physical body.[1] This ever-changing equilibrium is maintained by a dynamic process of feedback and regulation. *Tarot for the Healing Heart* takes a broader view of homeostasis—it is designed to keep you, your energy field, and your physical body in perfect order.

Whenever anything is out of balance in your energy field or physical body, the process of homeostasis automatically seeks to regain order. Most of this balancing system happens outside our awareness. For example, on a hot day, we perspire to cool off. Because we are losing body fluid, the thirst mechanism activates and tells us we need to drink water. When we replenish our fluids, the internal order is restored.

Another way to look at homeostasis is to think of it in terms of karma: an unseen law that adjusts wisely and intelligently each effect to its cause. Its action is perceivable and is the law of readjustment that restores disturbed equilibrium to the broken harmony of the world.[2]

On the individual level, as well as the universal, the law of karma is the principle of adjustment, balance, equilibrium, and harmony on all levels of being. It gives back to each person the actual consequences of the act, wisely adjusting each effect to its cause wherever disturbances occur.

The principle of adjustment to restore harmony can be called homeostasis or karma. Whatever you call it, the cyclical pattern of birth, growth, maturation, decay, death, and rebirth is the dance of illness and health—and the dance of life.

Choosing your karma: a tarot meditation

You are not a victim or puppet in your own life. The purpose of this meditation is to yield insights on how you can choose—and change—your karma. Pull the major arcana cards The High Priestess (No. 2), Justice (No.*) and Judgement (No. 20) from your tarot deck. Place them where you can clearly see the pictures without straining your eyes. The High Priestess represents inner knowing (intuition and feelings). Justice signifies outer knowing or the rational mind. Judgement is our system of checks and balances—or karma.

These three cards signify a relationship of healing energy expressed differently along the same spectrum. The number two represents balance or the need for balance. All three cards are the number two when reduced to a single digit: 11=1+1=2, 20=2+0=2. The focus of any number two tarot card is to stay in the middle—to maintain equilibrium or restore equilibrium.

---

* In some decks Justice is No. 8. For this meditation, it doesn't matter whether Justice is No. 8 or 11. Eight is nothing more than two taken four times.

The High Priestess removes the barrier between your inner and outer knowing. Her message is: "Have complete faith in your feelings. Pay attention to intuition." She is the gift of the inner knowing of the heart and she opens the door to mysticism. Her dreams are important; write them down. She recognizes that circumstances are always changing and that energy ebbs and flows. She remembers the past and compares the present to it. Her challenge is to formulate logical decisions and make judgments based on her trust of intuition.

Justice offers clarity of mind and a balanced intellect. It weighs and balances difficult questions and makes a decision based on detached fairness. An inner conscience makes adjustments and sets things right to establish balance and harmony. The message of Justice is: "What is out of balance? The search for equilibrium will restore order. The blending of the Higher Self with daily thinking produces harmony." Justice is the gift of a personal sense of right and wrong and the ability to set things right through fairness. It does not recognize, however, that impartial fairness can shut out compassion and mercy. The challenge of Justice is to accept personal responsibility for behavior and use the intuitive knowledge of The High Priestess in a practical way.

Judgement is an honest and sincere self-appraisal based on past actions. It is a time of reaping the harvest of past actions, for good or ill. Yes, it is a time to pay the piper, but the focus is on what is gained, rather than what is lost. It is the completion of the karmic cycle, and the outcome is a restoration of equilibrium, balance, and harmony for the Highest Good.

With Judgement, we ask where we have failed and succeeded and this results in understanding cause and effect. The message of Judgement is: "You are the initiator of your own change and development. You are responsible for yourself and the transformation (healing) of your life. You accept your personal power and the power you have to make choices. Is your inner judge merciful or harsh?"

The gift of Judgement is an increased awareness of the world based on taking responsibility for choices and actions. The miracle of Judgement is that by taking responsibility for our actions and choosing differently, we change karma. It is an all-embracing moment of truth when the heart looks on the personality with complete forgiveness. When we see ourselves with acceptance, we can accept others.

The challenge of Judgement is to change karma by blending inner and outer knowing, taking responsibility for our own actions, forgiving others and ourselves. Understanding cause and effect through the eyes of Judgement results in a compassionate restoration of order. Karma is not based on spiteful punishment, but an all-wise equilibrium that searches for the Highest Good.

Have your healing journal within reach. Begin by breathing in a slow, deep way. Breathe out the concerns of the day and breathe in a feeling of calm, peace, and well being. If your mind wanders, bring it back to your slow, deep breathing and the area around your heart where all healing takes place.

Gaze at The High Priestess. Let your focus soften the borders of the card. Notice her surroundings. Describe your sensations in detail. What is in her book? Touch the card and note any impressions you receive.

When you are familiar with The High Priestess, set the card in a place where you can see it and answer these questions in your journal, plus record any other insights you have: What is your intuition telling you? What do you need to remember from your past or your dreams in order to heal? What are The High Priestess' gifts to you? What are her challenges?

Repeat the above meditation using the Justice card and answer the following questions in your journal. (Be sure to include any thoughts you have and write without censoring yourself.) What needs to be set right for healing to occur? How can you use the intuitive knowledge of the High Priestess in a practical way for healing? What is your gift and challenge from Justice?

Meditate with the Judgement card as you did with the others. Answer the following questions in your journal: What action can you take in your own behalf to regain a sense of personal power? What choices can you make right now that will change karma? What is the gift of Judgement to you? What is the challenge?

By blending your inner and outer knowing (intuitive and rational self), you have started the process of healing and adjustment to restore harmony for the Highest Good, and, by doing so, you are choosing your own karma.

Picture the pain

To begin understanding your cycle of dis-ease and healing, try a layout called "Picture the Pain" (see figure 1, p. 36). It will help you gain insight into a specific illness, condition, or symptom. Know that the images you see in the layout reveal something important to you about your inner self. As with all tarot work, breathe deeply, center, and repeat the affirmation of healing, "I am calm, strong, and centered. I am at peace, safe and secure. I expect healing and I am thankful for it."

The illness and health meanings in chapter 8 are suggestions to unlock your intuition and start a dialogue between you and your Higher Self. They are not meant to be all-inclusive. Meditate upon a card, as described in the introduction, and let your inner wisdom guide you. Only you can determine what you need to do in order to heal. The following guide pertains to any tarot work found throughout the book:

Shuffle, cut the entire deck, and choose five cards face-down in any manner that pleases you. If space permits, place the layout on your healing altar. Keep the layout visible as you meditate and journal. You may want to photocopy the layout and put it in your journal. Write down and date your impressions. Leave the spread on the altar for a few days. Be patient, go slowly. Continue to enter insights about the layout in your journal. New information may surface over the next few days or even weeks.

As you shuffle, concentrate on where you are hurting. Picture your pain. Try to refrain from having preconceived notions about which cards will appear in your layouts. Chanting simple phrases as you shuffle, such as "Tarot, tarot, tell me true, what do I need to know from you?" can be powerful focal points and assist you in concentrating on the task at hand.

When you feel you have shuffled enough, choose five cards and place them according to figure 1 (p. 36), "Picture the Pain." Be sure the first card you draw is in position one, the second in position two, etc.

Now that you have a general reaction to the picture of your pain, go back to position one. Look at the cards and answer the following questions:

Card One—The pain: Listen to your body. What does the card's image tell you about your dis-ease? Does the card remind you of a past memory or current issue? Where might this pain be stored in your body?

Card Two—Awareness: Understanding is vital to healing. What insight do you have (hunch, intuition, feeling, gut reaction) right this moment that will help you heal?

Card Three—Unconscious hopes and fears (Blocks): The image on this card reveals that which is hidden from view and just beginning to surface. It signifies a block that has hindered your flow of energy. You may be vaguely aware of this information and it will soon become known to you in full, as you engage in the healing process.

What do you fear? What is holding you back? If the card is positive, it may represent your hidden desires, hopes, and dreams that you have not acted upon. This card may also be the major source of frustration in your life—that which is preventing you from becoming all you can be.

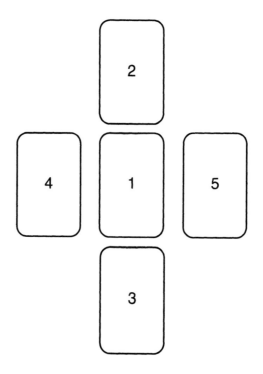

Figure 1
Picture the Pain

Card Four—The past: How has the flow of the past into the present affected your health? What factors in your personal history relate to feelings of dis-ease?

Card Five—The turning point: What is needed for healing? If the images on the card are negative to you, it is because they are graphic depictions of what is wrong. Once you see the problem clearly, you can begin to understand and heal it.

The broken heart

Illness reverberates through the four energy levels—physical, emotional, psychological, and spiritual. If dis-ease affects one level, eventually all levels will be out-of-ease. The following layout is called "The Broken Heart." The heart is tender and easily broken. It is also strong and the site of all healing. The Broken Heart tarot spread will help you understand how your particular condition is affecting you on all four planes of existence. The most important question to ask yourself now is, "How does my dis-ease affect me on the physical, emotional, psychological, and spiritual energy levels?"

Begin by shuffling the entire deck. Select five cards face down and place them in the Broken Heart configuration as shown in figure 2. Or, you can use your pain card (#1) from "Picture the Pain" and set it in position 1. This is helpful if you want more information about the last spread. Breathe deeply while you look at the cards and answer the following questions in your journal:

Position One—Heart of Darkness: The focus card, your dis-ease. What needs healing now? How does dis-ease (card 1) affect positions two, three, four, and five? This card carries the most weight in the reading and is central to interpreting the rest of the spread. All other cards are related to the focus of your dis-ease.

Position Two—Physical plane: Your body. How does dis-ease (card 1) express itself in your body? What is your body trying to tell you?

Position Three—Emotional plane: Your feelings. What emotions are problematic? How does dis-ease (card 1) emotionally express itself?

Position Four—Psychological plane: Your thoughts, ideas, thinking patterns, and decisions. How are your thought patterns expressed in symptoms? How does dis-ease (card 1) express itself psychologically?

Note: If a positive card shows up here, read it as problematic. For example, let's say The World (No. 21) appears. What could be negative about that? The world is your oyster, you have many good choices, right? Possibly not. The problem may be that you are overwhelmed by all the choices you now have and are frozen in indecision. Perhaps you are not ready to make your debut.

Position Five—Spiritual plane: Your connection to Spirit. How does your dis-ease (card 1) disconnect you from your own healing potential? How

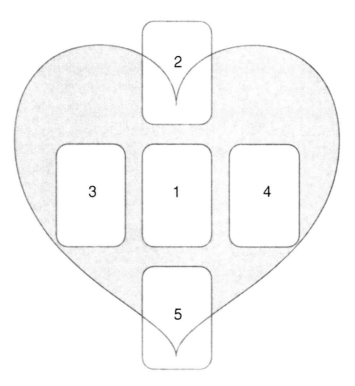

Figure 2
The Broken Heart

does it (card 1) block your creativity? Note: If you like the card in this position, it probably means you are not experiencing spiritual unrest at this time. Make an entry in your healing journal.

The blocked creativity of illness

When the universal life force—or creative energy—is experienced in a pure, unobstructed way, it creates health and happiness in our lives. When it is interrupted or distorted, it creates negative experiences and illness. Illness is a result of blocking the creative force, or as Barbara Brennan writes in *Light Emerging* (Bantam Books, 1993): "Illness is blocked creativity."[3]

I call the next layout "A Fresh Perspective of Dis-ease." It will give you insight into your illness—where the universal life force, or creativity, may be blocked. It will also bring about a more conscious awareness of yourself necessary for healing.

A fresh perspective of disease

As always, begin by deep breathing. As you exhale, say the word "relax" to yourself. Repeat the healing affirmation. Concentrate your attention on your body. Notice where there is pain and tension. Start with the face and picture the facial tension decreasing as you exhale and say the word "relax."

Proceed in this manner to relax other parts of your body. Breathe deeply. Next, relax your thought processes by saying, "I am calm, strong, and centered. All is well." Feel your worries lessen as you exhale and say "relax." When your mind has stopped racing, focus on what you are feeling. Note your emotions and let feelings go as you continue to breathe deeply and relax. Say, "I am at peace, safe and secure."

Experience the body, thought patterns and feelings as one unit, comfortable and relaxed. Say, "I expect healing and I am thankful for it." Using the entire tarot deck, shuffle the cards and randomly select one. Look at it and place it in position 1 as shown in figure 3 (p. 41). *This represents you now, at this one moment in time.* As you gaze at the card and experience the unity of mind, thought, and feeling, what new insight does the card give you about yourself? Let it become a symbol of a unified you—or a vivid depiction of where disharmony resides—and a place to begin.

You are comfortable and relaxed, alert in body, emotions, and mind. Imagine yourself to be in a natural setting that is attractive and serene. All is well. In this place of beauty, you are ready to review, in backward sequence, the chief events of your life.

Begin with this moment, then move to what you did earlier in the day, then to what happened yesterday. Work your way back to the time of your birth, or near it. Randomly select a card from the tarot deck and place it in position two as shown in figure 3. *This card represents your past.* As you meditate on the card, what from your past needs to be healed because it continues to cause dis-ease today?

Breathe deeply and say "relax" aloud. As you get closer to your inner self and the source of all-knowing, you become aware of a purple and white glow, which moves forward to meet you. There is nothing threatening about the experience. As the glow comes near you become aware of the details of its appearance. It is a loving being and you realize you are connecting to Spirit.

You stand face-to-face with this Wise Being, who begins to speak to you about the purpose of your life, the reasons for which you were born. Take time to allow for discussion and get in contact with the message that the Wise Being shares with you. Randomly draw a tarot card and place it in position three as shown in figure 3. *This card connects you to Spirit.* What new understanding about your life has come from this encounter with Spirit?

As you enjoy this quiet place of inner knowing, you are alert to what you have learned and begin to accept its meaning for your life. You now realize that the pattern of events in your life may have its origin in a realm beyond the scope of personal choice, as you have understood choice. You do one more life review in the context of what you learned from your encounter with Spirit. You see how the purpose of your life has been expressing itself all along. Your life events start to make sense.

Breathe deeply and draw a tarot card. Place it in position 4 as shown in figure 3. *This card allows you to soar to a higher overview of life.* It may give you hints about what future direction you need to take for self-healing. Knowing what you know

now about the patterns of your life, in what ways can you participate more fully with that purpose?

When the experience has completed itself, breathe deeply and slowly, and open your eyes. Wiggle your toes and touch the palms of your hands to the floor. Once you feel grounded and back in everyday existence, record the experience in your journal.

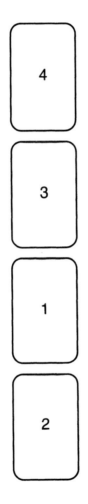

Figure 3
A Fresh Perspective of Dis-ease

Use the meanings of the tarot cards found in chapter 8 only as a guide. Let your inner wisdom guide you as you gain a fresh perspective of dis-ease.

Your health profile

Start keeping a health profile. Begin by recording every illness, accident, or symptom that has been significant in your life, and your age at the time it occurred. It may be easier if you start with today and work your way backward: adult, adolescent, child, toddler, baby. This will give you a broad overview of your life pattern of dis-ease.

Now connect your age and illness or accident with what was happening in your life. Give this a year's span—one year back from the onset of illness or the accident. When you have done this, add what you were feeling at the time. Your health profile might look something like mine:

HEALTH PROFILE

Age	Illness or Accident	Event	Feelings around event
4	rheumatic fever	death of grandmother	insecurity, fear, need for attention
12	hit by car while riding horse	told by mother that I wasn't mature enough to be out alone on back roads with horse	angry that I was being controlled, feelings of rebellion against authority

You will begin to see patterns emerge connecting illness/accident, to event, to feeling. My running themes surrounding dis-ease have always been fear and anger. Knowing your patterns will assist you in choosing self-help actions to safeguard you in future—and change your karma.

If you have a chronic persistent pain, another approach to the health profile is keeping a one-week event diary. Make a written daily log of your pain, the specific event or situation before the onset of pain, and your feelings at the time. Relate your symptoms to the situation and feeling. The daily log could look something like this:

DAILY LOG		
Date　Pain	Situation or event	Feelings
migraine headache stiff neck	death of my 15-year-old cat	Sadness, anger that he died, resistance to the flow of life, rigidity, not accepting his death

Choose a tarot card to represent your chronic pain and place it on the healing altar for the week. If you are unsure of which card to select, use a Sword. Many Swords have a knife-like, cutting, painful quality to them. Look at the card often or carry it with you throughout the day. Seeing the relationships between event/feelings/pain—and putting that relationship into symbolic form through tarot—will increase your conscious awareness of it.

By keeping a weekly log, I was able to see that I was not accepting the cycle of life and death, nor was I grieving. I was stuck in anger and rigid thinking. I selected the Ten of Swords as my pain card—the recognition that the end of a cycle had come and I needed to let go absolutely for growth to occur. When I allowed myself to cry, something I was taught *never* to do, the healing process of grief could begin and the headache/stiff neck subsided.

Now that you have an overview of illness, it's time to listen for the specific messages your body gives you about dis-ease. You will discover wounds, not defects. Chapter 4 begins by looking at the personal meaning of illness.

Notes to Chapter Three

1. *Taber's Cyclopedic Medical Dictionary.* 17th edition. Clayton L. Thomas, M.D., editor (Philadelphia: F. A. Davis Company, 1989), p. 909.

2. Haddick, Vern, Ph.D. "Karma and Therapy" from *Spiritual Healing.* Dora Kunz, editor (Wheaton, Ill.: Theosophical Publishing House, First Quest Edition, 1995), p. 184.

3. Brennan, Barbara Ann. *Light Emerging: The Journey of Personal Healing* (New York: Bantam Books, 1993), p. 317.

Chapter Four

THE HEART OF DIS–EASE: LISTENING TO THE MESSAGE

Look and you will find it.
What is unsought will go undetected.

Sophocles

Wounds, not defects

The defects and blocks that keep us from creating and living the life we want are not flaws and failures. They are wounds. As flaws and failures, we want to stamp them out or make them go away, but it is our very spirit we are severing or ignoring.

Sickness is a message from the heart that says something is out of balance and needs attention. Symptoms signal not a defect, but a wound exposed. The change in words from "defect" to "wound" shifts the focus of illness away from blame and shame.

Healing occurs within the divine act of loving ourselves. We cannot heal what we hate. Healing comes from tenderness: embrace the wounds, bandage them with loving care. They are the defining messages from your spirit asking you to become all you can be.

The personal meaning of illness

In order to learn from the deeper meaning of illness, we need to ask: What does this illness mean to me? Illness is a message from your body that says, "Something is out of balance. You are ignoring something important."

Dealing with the source of an illness usually requires a major life change. This change, or healing, leads to a life more connected to the spark of divinity in each of us. Sometimes the connection is called getting in contact with the Higher Self. My own term for it is "releasing the creative healer within."

Finding your personal meaning of dis-ease

In tarot, the Pages are associated with messages according to their individual suits: Page of Wands (inspirational or spiritual); Page of Cups (emotional or intuitive, messages from your dreams); Page of Swords (communications of all types, letters, e-mail, uncomfortable messages that require a decision); and Page of Pentacles (messages from your physical body, what your "gut instincts" are trying to tell you).

Try this: lay the four Pages out so you can clearly see them. Take the position—one card from either your "Picture the Pain" layout or the "Broken Heart" spread in chapter 3. Choose the card that calls for more information. Trust your intuition. The card you need to work with is the one you'll select. This card will be the focus of the meditation.

As you look at your focus card, ask yourself: What is my personal meaning of illness? Set it beside the Page of Wands and ask: What action must I take to initiate the healing process? What is the message from my creative healer within? Write your insights in your healing journal.

Next, place the focus card beside the Page of Cups. Ask what personal messages you are receiving through your emotions. What are your emotions trying to tell you? What types of dreams have you been having? Make an entry in your journal.

Take the focus card and set it near the Page of Swords. Ask how your dis-ease or discomfort has been communicated to you in words. Are the words you say to yourself loving or unloving? What decisions have you made recently that could contribute to feelings of imbalance?

The suit of Swords is a cutting suit, often associated with knife-like pain or surgery. What can be the meaning of any sharp pain you are having? Be sure to be examined by a health professional if you are experiencing severe pain. Record your insights in the journal and trust your reactions. Tarot is a truthful tool of growth and healing.

Finally, place the focus card next to the Page of Pentacles. Pentacles represent the physical body. What messages are you receiving from your body? Do you see any symbolism in the location of your pain? What do your instincts say?

No two illnesses are identical and no two healings are the same. You have now started to understand your personal meaning of illness. In the next section, we'll ride the roller coaster of emotions for more insight.

> *All these, however, were mere terrors of the night,*
> *phantoms of the mind that walk in darkness.*
>
> Washington Irving
> *The Legend of Sleepy Hollow*

Things that go bump in the night

This section introduces the connection between basic emotions—fear, anger, resentment—and the physical maladies they can produce. We learn fear early. From the moment of birth, we have the need for food, shelter, and love. If for any reason our needs are not met, we know fear. In normal function, fear is protective and beneficial. It keeps us safe.

The survival purpose of fear soon begins to permeate all aspects of our lives. We learn there is no endless source of anything. We are taught to live by the fear of loss. We align ourselves with fear: we fear someone will die, we fear we won't have enough money, we fear our significant relationships will dissolve or happiness won't last, we fear being alone—and we learn to fear illness. How will my life change? What will I lose by being ill? Fear of loss is where our fear of illness originates and where our resistance to change starts to grow.

"If I can but reach that bridge," thought Ichabod, "I am safe."
Washington Irving
The Legend of Sleepy Hollow

∾

The headless horsemen of dis-ease

Just as Ichabod Crane experienced unbridled terror from the headless horse-man, fear, anger, and resentment can gallop away with your health and happi-ness. The symbols of tarot carry a healing potential to transform your inner self. You can transform the baser feelings of fear, anger, and resentment into more elevated qualities of courage, love, and compassion.

Tarot can reframe your understanding of events, so just recognizing and naming a problem will actually start the healing process. By focusing on a lower vibration such as fear, anger, or resentment, you become established in that vibration. By focusing on a higher vibration such as courage, love, or compas-sion, you can establish yourself on that higher (healing) consciousness.

To discover what role these powerful basic feelings are playing in your life, try a layout called the "Headless Horsemen of Dis-ease." Remember you are work-ing with wounds, not defects. Be compassionate with yourself as you look at your woundedness.

Create an atmosphere of healing with anything that pleases you. When you feel relaxed, shuffle and cut the cards, using the entire deck. With the deck face down, choose four cards and place them according to the Headless Horseman layout in figure 4 (p. 49). Be sure the first card you draw is in position one, the second in position two, etc.

If you need more information for a specific position, shuffle the deck and pull another card or two. Place them next to the position that needs expansion. One or two more cards will explain the original single selection in more detail.

Position One—Fear: What am I afraid of losing? How is fear expressed in my physical body? Make an entry in your journal.

Position Two—Anger: What or who do I wish to punish? How is anger expressed in my physical body? Record your thoughts in the journal.

Position Three—Resentment: What emotion am I "re-feeling"? How is resentment expressed in my physical body? Make a journal entry about resentment.

Position Four—Advice Card: What action needs to be taken first to start the healing process? This card helps you focus your energy and gives you insight about where to concentrate your healing efforts.

Note: If the advice position is a court card (especially Queen or King), it strongly suggests consulting the health professional/healer of your choice.

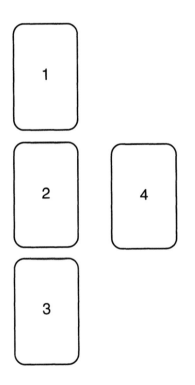

Figure 4

The Headless Horsemen of Dis-ease

Anger, resentment, and fear may not be major issues in your life, but they are basic feelings and most of us have had at least some experience with one or more of them. Make an entry in the healing journal about an instance when you felt anger, resentment, or fear. Do you recall any physical symptoms associated with the feelings? Try to make a mind-body connection with these basic emotions.

To experiment more with the mind-body connection, try an activity I call the posture of health and illness: Look at the pictures of tarot card figures. Select a few that intrigue you. Suspend your need for disbelief and pretend, for a moment, that you are that figure. Assume the position of the figure in the card. (*Caution:* Do not do this exercise if you have orthopedic problems. Do not do this exercise with No. 12, The Hanged Man—there is potential for neck, shoulder, and back injury.)

To get you started, assume the position of the Four of Pentacles. Now try No. 7, The Chariot. Note the difference in the way you feel between the two postures—the four of Pentacles is closed, The Chariot open. Now compare the squatting posture of The Devil (No. 15) to the dance of The World (No. 21). How and where do you feel these differences in your body? What does this mean to you when considering the inner processes of the mind-body connection? Play with several pairs of differing cards and make an entry in your journal about the mind-body connection in tarot.

Conscious mind—unconscious body

Does this mean that all illnesses originate in our minds? Well, yes, to the extent that the mind is intricately involved in the workings of the body. But, and this is a very important disclaimer, certainly not in the sense that we alone can control all the factors of illness and wellness.

We inherit genetic tendencies—alcoholism, diabetes, hemophilia, Huntington's chorea, hypertension, rheumatoid arthritis, schizophrenia, sickle cell anemia, and some forms of breast cancer are examples.[1] Our environment is composed of things that happen to us, such as childhood trauma and loss.

We are also exposed to toxic chemicals, pollution, and second-hand smoke. Our minds process personal experiences and lessons. All these interacting factors (genetics, environment, emotional trauma, personal choices, and experiences) give rise to illness.

Our conscious efforts to maintain health are sometimes unsuccessful, partial, or intermittent, at best. Certain conditions and situations really are out of our control.

If things are out of our control and we behave in foolish ways that interfere with our personal harmony, what's the point of books about healing? The unconscious body always seeks to maintain or restore inner harmony through homeostasis and karmic law. The conscious mind does not always feel obliged to follow the natural law of balance.

The point of healing is to bring the conscious mind into the same state as the unconscious body—harmony is maintained or restored by exploring the deeper meaning of illness through conscious choice and action.

Some factors, like personal choices, are in our control: a diabetic can choose to follow a prescribed diet; a person with high blood pressure can choose to quit smoking, lose weight, exercise, and decrease salt intake; an alcoholic can choose to refrain from the first drink. Through conscious choice, we can remember who we are and engage in the process of healing.

The mind-body connection tells us that the inner mental reality and the outer reality of the physical body are reflections of the same thing. Tarot card images can help us make that mind-body connection through the gateway of the unconscious. Yes, the use of tarot work in illness and healing will be limited, but the universal symbolism and relationships of tarot cards can also produce much-needed—and sometimes profound—insight. Choices and courses of action may become clearer through tarot work.

Working with tarot can have a soothing effect. Tarot's creative, positive energy can help us explore the emotional background of illness and will do no harm. The beauty is that it may do considerable good. Tarot allows us to step outside ordinary consciousness and look differently at the present moment. We can gain a new perspective and see life against an eternal backdrop. We can make the mind-body connection.

We work with tarot for clarity, discovery, knowledge, and to create desired results. When we use tarot to work through problems and formulate strategies, it takes on the character of therapy. *A word of caution here:* Tarot is a tool for insight, not a cure or a treatment. Seek professional counseling when you need it.

Life wisdom: listening to the message of dis-ease

Tarot for the Healing Heart makes no claim that illness is good or bad. Illness is a neutral message pointing us to the imbalances of daily life. Karmic law is always neutral. Illness offers insight about the choices we are making. I call the messages of dis-ease "listening to life wisdom."

When we feel pain or discomfort, be it physical or emotional, most of us want to rid ourselves of the effects as quickly as possible. In other words, we want to be healed with as little bother as possible. Healing, in this context, means elimination of symptoms, whether we seek traditional medical treatment or alternative forms of health care.

Sickness is markedly unpleasant and it is precisely this discomfort that causes us to look inside ourselves for answers and relief. If we allow introspection, we find truths about ourselves and the choices we've been making. When we allow for the deep inner experiences that illness can cause, we learn deep truths—we learn life wisdom. Think of life wisdom as an inner education that leads to personal growth and development.

Does this mean we have to avoid rapid healing in order to learn the message illness carries for us? *Not at all.* We can allow ourselves to be healed as quickly as possible—provided we understand the difference between an illness healed by external intervention and an illness healed because its message has been absorbed into our deep awareness. We can absorb its message and make better choices in the future. At that point, the illness may no longer be necessary.

What if the effects of an illness, accident, or injury are permanent? Healing can still take place, but it no longer means absence of symptoms. Used this way, healing becomes a move toward spiritual wholeness.

Because of the permanent effects of illness, accident, or injury, unexpected strengths and new possibilities are developed. These surprise developments may be the very message that the illness, accident, or injury was carrying. We may be forced to draw on strengths we never knew we had. Christopher Reeve, athletic actor, quadriplegic, and "superman" extraordinaire, comes to mind.

Unexpectedly, the permanent condition becomes a constructive element, in large part, because it was not eliminated. Healing has occurred in this case because the meaning of one's life is discovered. Learn to be open to the message of illness because you never know when the meaning will take shape and be embodied in your life because of it.

The heart of dis-ease: listening to the message in tarot

As always, begin tarot work by deep breathing to achieve a feeling of relaxation. Lay the Heart of Dis-ease spread on your healing altar for awhile so its entire message can be understood.

Using the entire tarot deck, shuffle and randomly select five cards from the face-down deck. Place them in positions one through five as shown in figure 5, the Heart of Dis-ease: Listening to the Message. Be sure that the first card you draw is in position one, the second in position two, etc.

> *Position One—The Heart of the Message:* most needs work now. This card is the key to understanding your message of dis-ease and serves as the focus card for positions two through five. (*Note:* If this is a court card, it may indicate consultation with a health care professional, healer, or therapist. Please see chapter 8 for details.) What is the key to decoding your message of dis-ease?

> *Position Two—Life Lesson:* What blocks your growth or prevents you from taking loving action in your own behalf? What is your life lesson? How does this relate to card one, the heart of the message?

> *Position Three—Revolving Door:* What illness or symptoms do you have that keep repeating themselves? What do you gain when you feel ill? How does this relate to the heart of your message in card 1?

Position Four—Seeking the Healing Cycle: What types of losses (due to illness) make you want to seek the healing cycle? How does this insight relate to the heart of the message in card 1 (your priority)?

Position Five—Life Wisdom: What unexpected strengths and new possibilities open up as a result of listening to the message of dis-ease? How does the heart of the message, card 1, relate to these unforeseen, surprise developments?

Keep the layout on your altar for a few days. Be patient. The answers will come.

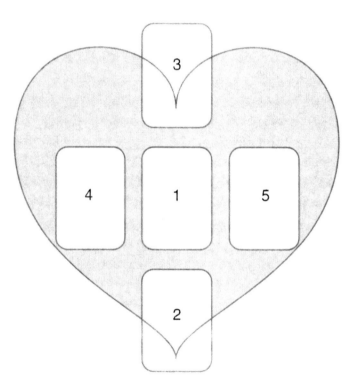

Figure 5
The Heart of Dis-ease: Listening to the Message

The Bridge

There is a land of the living and a land
of the dead and the bridge is love.
Thornton Wilder

In the movie *Patch Adams*, Robin Williams' character offers us insight into illness, healing, and death. Paraphrased, he says that if we treat the disease, we win or lose. If we treat the whole person, we always win, regardless of the outcome.

I cannot write a book about healing without exploring the subject of death. I propose that physical handicap or illness does not interfere with our capacity to give and receive love. In my years as a registered nurse, I cared for many patients near death and I saw profound healing: relationships with estranged family members were mended, gravely ill patients were able to put their lives in perspective and make sense of it all, spiritual peace was found.

Many of my dying patients wondered why they still had so many visitors. As a young nurse, I didn't know the answer to that question, but I do now: their spirits were still very much alive. Spirit and love attracted others because the others saw life, not death, and they were comfortable in the presence of love.

No matter our condition, to choose love is to bring into effect the spiritual healing force and source of life. The secret to being eternal is the capacity to give and receive love.

Even with a spiritual view of death, the truth is people die and we are left to pick up the pieces. Some of us have unfinished business with the deceased: regrets, anger, pain. A gap is left when someone dies, regardless of the quality of relationship. We can have feelings of rage, despair, or sadness.

It is not in the scope of *Tarot for the Healing Heart* to discuss afterlife, reincarnation, Avalon, the underworld, Summerland, or any other term meaning life after death. My purpose is to help you *now*, in *this life*. If you are afraid of death, the next meditation will help you gain insight into your fear. Be open to your power and capacity to heal through love.

Letting go of fear: a meditation with the Death card

The Death card, No. 13, traditionally means transformation, rebirth, letting go, and permanent change. It rarely signifies physical death, but for the purposes of this meditation, that is exactly what it means—coming to terms with your own mortality.

When you are able to accept your own death as inevitable, you gain a broader perspective of your life direction and the choices you are now making. Priorities become clearer and change is easier to make. The Death card meditation will assist you in understanding that the secret to being eternal is the capacity to give and receive love.

Pull from your tarot deck No. 13, the Death card. Sit comfortably and prop the card up in front of you. Allow the edges of the card to soften in your gaze. Concentrate on slow deep breathing.

As you gaze at Death, think about your own death. To get you started, answer the following questions: What does dying mean to you? Are you afraid to die?

Pretend you are writing your own obituary. Let your whole life pass before you. How do you want to be remembered? What are your accomplishments? What gives your life real meaning and purpose? What is the one thing you wish you could do that you have not yet done?

What has been the most significant death in your own life? If you have not experienced the death of a close friend or loved one, anticipate how you would feel if a significant person in your life dies tomorrow. What do you fear most about this death? Record all your insights into your healing journal.

We can't force ourselves to let go of fear of death, but by understanding how fear operates in our lives, we have a greater chance of releasing it. When we operate from a fear-based philosophy, it is difficult to give and receive love. In fear, love becomes possession and fear of loss controls our actions.

Somewhere along the way, we become fearful of death. When we operate out of fear, we set up the wrong life. When fear is released, we are then in a position to give and receive love without hidden agendas. By letting go of fear we choose a healing cycle—to become who we truly are instead of who we think we ought to be—and that's the true meaning of dying in order to be reborn.

Good grief

The causes of sorrow vary and loss takes many forms. All change involves loss. We experience loss not only with the death of a loved one, or a pet, but with events like divorce, ending a significant relationship, loss of a body part after surgery, changing careers, losing a job, or moving to a new town.

The list of losses is endless. Often, our situations reflect a whole pattern of loss, which has gone on throughout life. Grief is a necessary process that allows us to heal, find new strength, and carry on with our lives in a meaningful way. Good grief moves us forward after any loss.

Unresolved grief can have a devastating affect on our health. Physical manifestations of unresolved grief include, but are not limited to: sleep disorders, loss of appetite or binge-eating, being more accident-prone, social withdrawal, thoughts of suicide, confusion, hallucinations, lethargy, muscle weakness, shortness of breath, extreme fatigue, angry outbursts, depression or despair, loneliness, and a hollow yearning.[2] Needless to say, unresolved grief is a painful place to be that can cause prolonged illness and interfere with the healing process.

Learning to cope and find meaning after loss is not an easy journey. The way is filled with hills and valleys. For true healing to occur, you may need professional help to decrease stress, anxiety, and feelings of powerlessness. Never be ashamed that you need professional guidance during a time of loss. By reaching out, you are taking loving, healing action on your own behalf and that is not an act of weakness. It takes tremendous courage to face the pain of loss directly and initiate change.

The goal of any grief counseling should help you learn how to: accept the loss without denial; experience the pain of grief in a safe way; adjust to the new environment without the deceased (or with the loss); withdraw emotional energy from the loss and focus it elsewhere in a constructive way; say your goodbyes (let go); and, move on to a new and different life.[3]

Most people who work with tarot for any length of time find it takes on the character of therapy. A tarot reading can help us work through the loss, explore intuition, and formulate coping strategies, much like psychoanalysis. Used this way, tarot emphasizes emotional and psychological healing. When emotions and outlook improve, the physical symptoms of grief will quietly go away.

The following layout, called "Good Grief," can be used alone or in conjunction with traditional forms of grief counseling. The two need not contradict one another. Each is valuable. Each offers unique insights. I have placed the Good Grief spread in this chapter because the physical symptoms of grief carry profound messages for change, but often go unrecognized and untreated. Listening to the messages of grief can put you in a healing cycle—if you understand the language of loss.

Begin your layout by breathing deeply to create a feeling of relaxation and centeredness. It may be helpful to have a symbol of your loss nearby to use as a focus point as you do the spread. The symbol can be a picture of the person or pet you are grieving, a business card from your former worksite, a gift that your beloved gave you, a piece of jewelry or family heirloom, a picture of you before your surgery or accident, anything at all that symbolizes the specific loss.

Decorate your healing altar in black, if this feels right to you, to symbolize death of the old and letting go. Purple signifies profound healing. You may want to burn black candles to release negativity, or white for pure intention. A heavy incense such as vanilla, jasmine, opium, or narcissus connects you to the spirit of death and rebirth, as do dark stones such as black obsidian or onyx. Crystal amethyst speaks of spiritual healing. Your own intuition works best because no ritual you do is sacred unless it is sacred to you.

Stand or sit before the healing altar and say words that seem appropriate to you, according to your own spiritual tradition. Ask your healing guide to be with you if this pleases you. Say affirmations aloud to signal your pure intention, but remember that your own words work best. You can say something like this:

> I ask that the Dark Goddess (or your name for the spirit of death and
> rebirth) bless and protect me during this reading. I ask for wisdom,

guidance, and comfort as I deeply mourn my losses. I release the past with love and I am free to live my life. I expect healing and I am thankful for it. This is correct and for the good of all, may it harm none.

The good grief spread

Shuffle the cards and randomly select nine cards. Using the order in which you drew them (first card is position one, second card is position two, etc.), place the cards in positions one through nine as shown in figure 6, the Good Grief layout (p. 61). Turn them over and record your initial overall impression of the spread. You are looking at a picture of your grief. Does it surprise or frighten you? Why or why not?

Positions one and two are related and read together: Position one is a life lesson of grief—*Symptoms:* What are your physical symptoms of grief and loss? How does grief express itself in your body? Please refer to the section titled "Good Grief" for a list of grief symptoms, but don't limit yourself to it. Any subtle (and not so subtle) discomfort that you suspect is grief-related probably is. Another way to determine grief ailments is to think of conditions that appeared only after your loss.

Position two is a healing cycle of grief—How can you experience the pain of grief in a healing way? The second card is the solution to your symptoms. To make the physical discomfort subside, grief needs to express itself constructively through open acknowledgment of the loss and permission to grieve. What healing action can you take in your own behalf to feel better physically? If you need more information for this, or any position, draw another card and read the two together. Please refer to chapter 8.

Positions three, four, and five are related and should be read together: Position three is neutral information—*the facts of your loss.* What concrete details surrounding your loss do you know to be true? What is the true nature of your loss? For example, if you were fired, what events in your company led up to your dismissal? If a loved one died in an accident, how did events come together to result in the accident, such as bad brakes, fatigue, or alcohol?

Position four is a life lesson in grief—your thoughts about the loss: What does this loss mean to you? What do you think about at 3 A.M.? Where are you conflicted? What are the important decisions that need to be made, or where is your indecision? What negative self-talk do you tell yourself? How has the loss affected you psychologically? Can you look at the facts from position three and see how they may have become part of a distorted thinking pattern? Are you thinking clearly about what you need to do next?

Position five is the healing cycle of cards 3 and 4: How can you accept the loss and enter a healing cycle? What do you need to do about the facts of the case and your thought patterns to enable you to accept the loss without denial? What action will allow you to change your thought patterns? If it is a court card, especially a Queen or a King, it may indicate the need for counseling. Swords may indicate the need to keep a journal or see a lawyer. Wands point to the need for a creative outlet or hobby. Cups may mean emotional work with a counselor or spiritual adviser, drawing your family close or keeping a dream journal. Pentacles tell you to pay attention to your health and financial security. The major arcana suggest a spiritual search, both formally and informally.

Positions six and seven are related and should be read together. Card 6 is a life lesson of grief—Emotions and feelings: What are you feeling about your loss? Anger? Fear? What are your emotions? Resentment? Worry? Despair or depression? Have you had psychic visions? Describe them. What does your intuition tell you about the loss? How do these feelings and emotions manifest themselves in your daily life? Headaches, insomnia, ulcers, high blood pressure, irritability, impatience, temper, etc.? How much of your emotional energy are you investing in the loss? How much time do you spend feeling uncomfortable emotions? How have your emotions restricted your activities?

Position seven is the healing cycle of grief—Withdrawing emotion from the loss: What actions do you need to take to get your life back? What do you need to do to spend less time feeling uncomfortable? How can you withdraw your emotional energy from the situation? Where do you need to invest your emotional energy to create a healing cycle and, once again, experience joy? Please refer to position five and chapter 8 for hints on what the cards are trying to tell you, but use them as launching points. Your spiritual self knows what needs to be done so you can let go of the pain and enter a healing cycle.

Positions eight and nine are related and should be read together. Card 8— Support for the healing process: This card tells you where to find healing

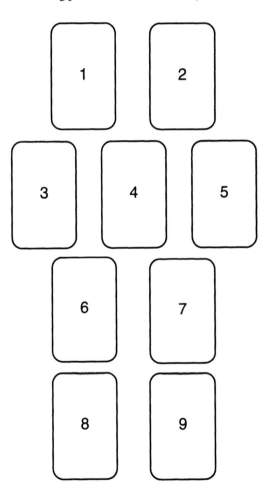

Figure 6
The Good Grief Spread

support. Even if it is a card traditionally associated with negative meanings, read it in a positive way. For instance, let's say the Devil, No. 15, appears here. In this position it would mean the need to lighten up and play, to be "devilish." The Four of Pentacles, usually connected to miserliness, would suggest the need to set boundaries and conserve your energy.

Position nine is a healing cycle of grief—Adjusting to the new environment without the deceased or with the loss: What actions will allow you to move on with your life despite your loss? Do you need to move? Change the furniture? Look for a job? Take a class? Get counseling? Give items to charity that belonged to the deceased? Do you need to perform a grief ritual?* What housekeeping—mental, emotional, spiritual—needs done so you can enter a new and different life?†

If you are unclear about the cards, keep the layout on the healing altar for a few days and record any additional insights as they occur to you in the journal. Grieving has its own timetable and cannot be rushed. Take all the time you need to heal. Chapter 6, "The Heart of Healing," offers more information about support for the healing process.

When you are ready to move on, you may want to change the items on the altar to reflect healing: replace the dark candles with white, blue or purple, use a light incense, or rose, to symbolize the universal healing force of love. Make your altar a physical expression of your own spirituality and let your intuition be your guide.

---

* For more information on performing a mourning rite (or grief ritual), please refer to my first book, *Tarot Shadow Work* (Llewellyn Publications, 2000), chapter 6, "Embracing Your Shadow: Discovering the Light Within," section titled "Moving On."

† As with all layouts in *Tarot for the Healing Heart,* not every question will apply to you. Select one or two that ring true and work with them first. If a question stimulates you to contemplate another area of your life, follow your inspiration.

Notes to Chapter Four

1. Harvey, A. McGehee, M.D., et. al., *The Principles and Practice of Medicine* (New York: Appleton-Century-Crofts, 1980), pp. 439–444.

2. *Healing and the Grief Process*, Lynn Keegan, editor (Boston: Delmar Publishers, 1997), p. 19.

3. Akner, Lois F., C.S.W., *How to Survive the Loss of a Parent: A Guide for Adults* (New York: William Morrow and Company, 1993), pp. 107–109.

PART THREE

HEART AND SOUL

What lies behind us and what lies before us are tiny matters, compared to what lies within us.

Ralph Waldo Emerson

Chapter 5

THE OPEN HEART:
UNDERSTANDING HEALING

*Learn to get in touch with the silence within yourself
and know that everything in this life has a purpose.*
Elisabeth Kübler-Ross

Health attracts health

Our emotional and physical health is closely related to our attitudes about ourselves and life in general. When we feel good about ourselves we allow good things to happen in our lives. When we don't love ourselves, we permit an opening for negative experiences to come our way. Every cell in our body is aware of our emotions and thoughts, and responds to their energy.

At the deepest cellular level, all negative emotions and thoughts have a negative effect on the body. These energies, coupled with their impact on bodily systems, will sooner or later present themselves as ill health because they are states of imbalance. The good news is positive energy also affects all levels of our being—but in a balanced, harmonious way. Health attracts health.

The inner journey of healing: paying attention to intuition

The wisewomen crones of long ago used their intuitive minds for healing, and instinctively knew that healing was "to make whole"—body, mind, and spirit needed to be as one for healing to occur. They saw the interconnection of all things—plants, animals, people, and the earth's cycles were all part of the same connected natural world.

Intuition is one of your greatest assets in healing work. The ability to listen to and hear your inner guidance is a gift and we all have the gift of intuition if we but listen to its voice. Like all abilities, an intuitive mind requires care, attention, and practice to become fully developed.

Many good books are available about the development of intuition. My favorite is *The Psychic Pathway* by Sonia Choquette (Crown Trade Paperbacks, 1995). Treat yourself to a bookstore visit and let an intuitive guiding force lead you to your correct path of learning.

You may want to keep a journal of intuitive insights so that, over time, you can observe the accuracy of your impressions. By seeing your intuitive processes on paper, you will learn to listen to and trust the information you receive from your still small voice—and the still small voice belongs to the healer. Later on, you will learn how to awaken this healer within.

Healing as a lifestyle

The reward for paying attention to intuition is healing. Starting your day with an *awareness* of your intuitive powers helps you to heal yourself and others. How many times, despite your best efforts, do you start your day in chaos? The kids are late, the cat didn't come home, the zipper is broken, the coffee cups are dirty, and the radio blares that traffic is snarled. This is not a good way to start a day of healing.

If we are too busy to feel, we are too busy to be aware, and "busyness" narrows our awareness, not expands it. Some of the least perceptive people I know are that way because they are in such a rush. If we are too busy to stop and notice—to listen to the small voice that only whispers and can't be heard above the din of everyday life—we can't develop intuitive awareness.

I'm not suggesting that we "drop out" of life. Quite the contrary—the more aware we are of our inner needs and desires through intuition, the more focused and productive we become because we go about our work with enthusiasm.

Restoring our lives to balance is no easy task. Women are often required to focus on many tasks at one time. We try to balance careers, children, relationships, and responsibilities. By focusing on the necessary, we can give up being all things to all people. By simplifying, quieting down, creating room for the sacred, we regain balance and reclaim our healing heritage.

We are free from the exhaustion caused by setting up the wrong life. By finding the time to be still, a great irony occurs—out of the calm, a tremendous healing energy allows us to charge ahead with renewed spirit and focus, and we start setting up the life we were meant to live.

Try this: Arise thirty minutes earlier in the morning and begin your day differently, with the intention to heal. Become protective of your healing time. Small, loving acts that you do for yourself form the basis of intuitive health. When you first get up, stretch and look out the window. *Take the time* to notice the trees, sky, clouds, and sun.

Light a candle on your healing altar to connect your spirit to earth, moon, and sky (but be sure to extinguish the candle before leaving your home for the day). Say your personal affirmation out loud so the universe knows of your intention to heal. Breathe deeply. Have a glass of juice or great-tasting tea.

Now, before you turn on the radio for the blaring bad news of the day, or the rest of the household awakens and demands your attention, what will you do for yourself for the next twenty minutes? Only you can decide what will teach you to get in touch with the silence inside.

You will discover that an amazing thing happens when you devote the beginning of each day to intuitive healing: protected by this loving energy, you will have the necessary coping skills and stamina to get the kids ready, find the cat, fix the zipper, wash the coffee cups, and make your way to work.

Meditation for the inner healing journey

Personal qualities that enhance the healing process include patience, faith, trust, and intuition.[1] Patience is the ability to slow down and is symbolized by the suit of Pentacles, the physical plane of healing. Faith is an emotional belief in a power greater than oneself and invites assistance and support from the universal healing force. Faith corresponds to the suit of Cups, the emotional plane of healing.

Trust calls for a conscious decision to continue with a healing lifestyle, even when no energy shift is apparent. The suit of Swords represents trust, the psychological, mental plane of healing. Intuition is the still small voice within that always knows what is best for us, sometimes referred to as the Higher Self. Intuition is related to the suit of Wands, the spiritual, creative aspect of healing on the plane of everyday actions.

In this meditation, the Aces of each suit represent the four qualities of healing: Pentacles (patience), Cups (faith), Swords (trust), and Wands (intuition). Notice the artwork of the four Aces in your tarot deck. Can you see that each Ace offers a gift? (The Aces shown here on page 71 are from the *Golden Dawn Magical Tarot*, Llewellyn Publications.)

Separate the four Aces from your tarot deck. Place them on the altar according to the diagram in figure 7, p. 72. The number seven symbolizes inner work, so set a candle by each Ace and put the other three candles where they please you. If you have only one candle, place it in the middle of the circle of Aces and remember—your *intention* to heal is the most important quality you bring to any activity in this book.

Breathe deeply to achieve a feeling of relaxation. Look at the Ace of Swords and ask it for the gift of illumination, to enhance your mind and intellect. Light the Ace of Swords candle. Feel the element of air cleanse away any blockages of your mind. Ask the Ace of Swords for trust and the ability to continue with a healing lifestyle, even when no energy shift is apparent. In other words, when no results are immediately felt or observed.

Allow any thoughts to float through your mind; acknowledge them and release negative thoughts by breathing through your mouth. Stay with the Ace of Swords' gifts for as long as you like and give thanks when you are done.

The Ace of Swords

The Ace of Wands

The Ace of Cups

The Ace of Pentacles

Look at the Ace of Wands and ask it for the gift of inspiration and creativity, to give you the courage you need to heal and attune to your life purpose. Light the Ace of Wands candle. Feel the element of fire burn away any dis-ease you are carrying.

Ask the Ace of Wands for intuition and the ability to hear your still small voice of inner wisdom. Do not censor the impressions, for they come from the sacred space of your Higher Self. Stay with the Ace of Wands' gifts for as long as you like and give thanks when you are done.

Look at the Ace of Cups and ask it for the gift of emotional clarity, to give you a healing heart. Light the Ace of Cups candle. Feel the element of water wash every part of your mind, body, and spirit and renew you with clear emotions.

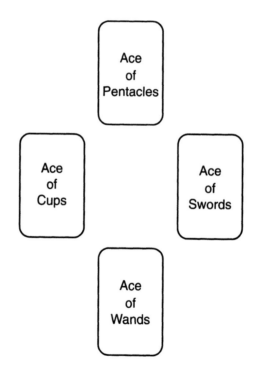

Figure 7

Inner Healing Journey: Meditation with the Four Aces

Ask the Ace of Cups for the emotional faith in a power greater than yourself and invite support from the universal healing force. If you feel like crying, allow the tears to flow, for it is often the key to inner healing. Stay with the Ace of Cups' gifts for as long as you like and give thanks when you are done.

Look at the Ace of Pentacles and ask it for the gift of abundance, to give you everything you need to heal and a sense of everything you value. Light the Ace of Pentacles candle. Feel the element of earth providing you with strength, security, and your own sense of power.

Ask the Ace of Pentacles for patience, the ability to slow down, to listen to the messages of dis-ease, and for a strong, healthy body. Close your eyes and become aware of your body. What does it feel like to be in it right now? Breathe in a feeling of stamina and wellness. Breathe out pain, stiffness, and any tensions of the day. Stay with the Ace of Pentacles' gifts for as long as you like and give thanks when you are done.

Continue to breathe deeply. Slowly become aware of the room and pay special attention to your body. Notice if anything has changed. Place your hands on the chair, earth, or floor, and move your feet to ground your energy. If you feel lightheaded, breathe deeply and keep your hands grounded until you return to normal consciousness. Eating a complex carbohydrate such as whole grain bread, potatoes, or cereal will also help ground the energy.

Make an entry in your journal. What happened to you during the inner journey of healing? You may want to keep the four aces on the altar for further contemplation. You can either extinguish the candles now or let them burn down completely. As always, be aware of fire safety.

The open heart: understanding healing

With the foundation of self-love, the clear intent to heal, and an attitude of detachment and acceptance, we can begin to understand healing with an open heart. In a tarot layout called "The Open Heart," you will be able to assess the personal basis of all healing—the art of loving yourself.

Begin by breathing deeply to achieve a state of relaxation. Visualize yourself in a state of perfection. Repeat the affirmation (the intent) to heal: "I am calm, strong, and centered. I am at peace, safe and secure. I enjoy who I am. I expect healing and I am thankful for it."

Shuffle the entire deck and lay out five cards as shown in figure 8 (p. 75). Be sure the first card drawn is in position one, the second in position two, etc. If you need more information for any one position, simply draw another card as the "advice card" and lay it next to the position in question.

Breathe deeply to retain a sense of detachment and acceptance to the results of the Healing Heart spread. Remember that you may be looking at wounds, but your woundedness and any difficulty loving yourself are not defects. You are exactly where you need to be at this time in your life. Being in a life lesson is an honorable choice.

Begin reading position one—the heart of self-love: What is at the center of the art of self-love? How can I open my heart to healing?

If the card appears negative to you, it may be a clear depiction of self-destructive acts.* This negative card will help you understand where you are unkind and unloving to yourself, thereby blocking the healing process. Key to loving yourself is an understanding of where you are currently unloving. You don't know what you don't know, and this first position may provide you with much-needed insight. It is the center or focus of the entire spread.

Position two—the spiritual expression of self-love: How can self-love be expressed spiritually? What does the "healer within" tell me about ways to love myself? How does this card relate to card 1? The Hierophant, High Priestess, or King/Queen of Wands suggest the need for a spiritual adviser of choice.

If this card feels negative to you, it is a description of being cut off from the voice of Spirit. For example, if The Devil (No. 15) appears, it can signify the boundary of fear. The message of this card would be to examine the role of fear in your life. By coming to terms with your fear,

---

* All cards carry messages for growth and every card presents us with an opportunity to learn and change. A card will feel "negative" or uncomfortable (challenging), or "positive" and reassuring (showing our strengths).

you will no longer be bound to it and your spirit will be able to express itself in loving, healing, creative ways.

Position three—the mental expression of self-love: What thought processes are loving? What negative self-talk keeps me from loving myself? How can I change the things I tell myself so that health attracts health?

A card that feels positive will point you toward healing. It tells you what to keep in your life and where you are strong on the mental plane. A negative feeling card will tell you where you need to work and what needs attention. If a court card appears, especially the Knight, Queen, or King of Swords, a counselor or therapist may be indicated to help you sort out your thinking patterns. How does this card relate to card 1, the heart of healing?

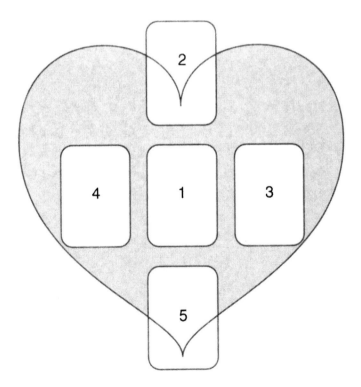

Figure 8
The Open Heart

Position four—emotional expression of self-love: What is the emotional expression of loving myself? Am I emotionally invested in illness? How does position four relate to card 1, the heart of healing?

We cannot heal what we hate. If this card feels negative, you are looking at the part(s) of you that you hate and that need the most attention now. How does self-hatred manifest itself in your life? If the card feels positive, it tells you what to keep, grow, and nurture in the art of loving yourself. A Knight, Queen, or King of Cups strongly suggests the need for a counselor/ healer to help you sort through conflicting/ confusing emotions that could be blocking your emotional healing.

Position five—the physical expression of self-love: How can I best love my body? Ask yourself: How does this card relate to position one, the heart of healing? What do I need to understand about loving my body?

If the card feels negative, it points you toward lifestyle or health habits that are hurting you and gives you a glimpse of what you need to change to really love your body. If the card feels positive, it tells you what to keep and where you are strong. The King or Queen of Pentacles suggests the need for a healer or health professional. Get a check-up.

Make an entry in your journal about the art of loving (and nurturing) yourself. You may want to keep the Open Heart layout on the healing altar for a few days and make additional entries in the journal. Go slowly. It will take time to change old habits that are no longer useful to you.

The healer within

There are three distinct categories of healing energy:

1. Personal energy generated by the body.

2. Mental energy, the ability to focus the mind and direct energy through thought.

3. Spiritual or mystical energy, working with Spirit and the power of prayer.

For those who have a strong personal energy and have developed good mental skills, it can be a challenge to go beyond the personal and ask for the God's or Goddess' help.

Using only your personal energy to heal limits the scope and amount of energy available to do the healing. Using only your mental power makes you susceptible to fatigue and tension headaches when you concentrate your mind and focus your attention. Working with mystical (or psychic) energy means the energy source is limitless. By requesting and using the universal healing force, you open yourself up to a much higher (and stronger) level of energy. When you allow yourself to step aside and let the universal force flow naturally through you, the healing that occurs is far beyond what you would normally believe to be possible.

The key to opening ourselves to this beautiful loving light is through quieting the mind, centering, and focusing our attention on it. With focused intent and practice, (using the methods suggested in this book), *anyone* can learn to attune to this higher consciousness. It is within—and available to *all* who seek it.

Spirit is subtle and often overlooked by those who aren't paying attention. If your mind is preoccupied with brain-numbing busyness, you are going to miss your cues. The requirement for this most mystical and subtle experience of universal love is the act of *surrendering* yourself to it—to the images and experiences governed by the heart, rather than the mind.

Look and listen with full awareness—not to others, but to your own inner voice. Slow down, breathe deeply, center, meditate, pray, follow your intuitive voice, and engage in sacred play. Ask freely for what you need, trust that you will receive it, *expect healing*—then relax, knowing that guidance is on the way.

Temperance: the healing angel

Tarot author Mary K. Greer calls Temperance, No. 14, the "healing angel." In her groundbreaking book *Tarot for Your Self* (Newcastle Publishing, 1984), she describes Temperance as an archetypal healer and "The Alchemist." Temperance is your personal physician who can prescribe the actions and "medicine" necessary to heal yourself.

Temperance has one foot on land, depicting rational thought and one foot in water, representing the flow of emotions. She or he symbolizes the need for continual flow and movement of feeling to prevent stagnation—emotions striving for balance.

In Temperance, we learn how to balance conflicting emotions (joy and sorrow, anger and love), by allowing these emotions to flow between higher consciousness and conscious awareness—producing an integration of feeling and thought. Temperance is a graceful transition between human problems (disease) and the divine illumination required to solve them—healing.

When emotions are not allowed to flow, they get stuck, or blocked. By either sinking into depression or erupting in violence, illness results. Undue weight given to any one emotion will injure them all. By allowing the higher self to flow freely with the rational mind, we find a balanced harmony and a supreme center. By meditating with Temperance, we can open ourselves to a universal wisdom and a belief that heals.

Contacting the healer within

Separate Temperance, No. 14, from your tarot deck. Place the card where you can see it clearly without straining your eyes. Perform any ritual that pleases you and feels sacred, be it lighting candles, playing soft music, or burning incense. By creating a special atmosphere, you are cuing your unconscious that something important is about to happen.

Allow the borders of the card to soften. In your mind's eye, step inside the Temperance card to be with your healing angel. Let her come near you.* She reaches out to you and you can feel her strength, balance, and compassion. You are completely calm and relaxed in her presence.

She spreads her arms above you and sends a gentle shower of healing energy to you in a loving, protective sphere. The healing energy has all the colors of a subtle rainbow and you realize the rainbow's hues reflect your own changing emotions. The colors of the rainbow and your emotions mix and blend, just as

---

*   Your healing angel may be male, female, or androgynous. It simply doesn't matter as long as you are comfortable with the angel's presence.

flowing water mixes and blends. For the first time in your life, you feel yourself to be a flowing, ever-changing, perfect part of a greater picture. Stay with the feeling of balance, harmony, and centeredness for as long as you like.

Continue deep breathing. From this state of calm centeredness, locate any pain that is within your body and place your hands over it. Stay with the pain for a moment and experience your thoughts and feelings.

Pay special attention to your emotions. Explore your emotions around the pain while being cradled in your healing angel's wings. Consider the things you desire and the things you dread. Are you consciously aware of blocking feelings? As you find that feeling, connect it to your pain.

When you are ready, move your awareness to the healer who has always been inside of you. Here is your wisdom and your light. Feel the calm centeredness. Move back to the pain and feel the discord. Continue shifting from calm and discord, calm and discord, until they get closer together and, finally, merge as one.

When you feel calm and balanced, ask the healer within: What do I need to release for the healing energy to flow? Stay with the healer within until a sense of peace fills you. Do not try to force answers. The answers will come in their own way and in their own time.

Reach up to the part of yourself that has always known your highest good. You are the person who knows how to heal yourself better than anyone else. You are the healer within. Give yourself plenty of time to integrate the relationships between your pain and your feelings. Move back and forth from the human with pain to the healer with universal power, until you feel completely merged. Affirm your clear intent to seek balance, change, and take the necessary actions to heal.

Temperance once more showers you with the gentle energies of healing. Her robes intermingle with the delicate colors of the rainbow. She sends healing energy to every part of your body and stays a bit longer where you have placed your hands. You feel all pain leave and a calm inner harmony replaces any discord.

As you thank her, she says she lives within you—and always has. Her healing power is available to you for the honest asking of it—the only requirement is a willingness to accept her gifts in whatever forms they take.

When you are ready, step out of the borders of the Temperance card and allow the edges to become two-dimensional once more. Breathe deeply, wiggle your feet, and place your hands on the chair or floor to ground the energy. Rise slowly and stretch. If you still feel lightheaded, drink a glass of water or eat a complex carbohydrate like wholegrain bread. Make an entry in your journal about contact with the healer within. In what way has the healing angel changed your sense of personal power?

The cycle of healing: whatever goes around comes around

Pain both originates from and affects your physical, emotional, psychological, and spiritual being. The healing process is more involved with getting obstacles out of the way, rather than pulling up creative energy. Once the blocks are gone on all four levels, healing energy flows from inside us like a bubbling spring—and the pain subsides or becomes manageable because it is understood.

Healing is a cyclical process that carries us on a spiral of learning. What is the message of dis-ease and healing? Each cycle requires more self-acceptance and more change as we go deeper and deeper into ourselves. All dis-ease requires change from within to facilitate healing, and all change requires a type of giving up or surrender—whether it be a habit like smoking, a physical capability or organ, a stress-filled job, a destructive lifestyle, or a fear-based belief system.

In healing, we release resentment, despair, conflict, and fear. We receive acceptance, strength, peace of mind, and love—especially self-love. This process of releasing and receiving brings us back to the process of homeostasis described in chapter 3—a wonderful system of checks and balances designed to keep us in perfect working order.

Our balancing system, or homeostasis, serves to take care of us on all four levels: physical, emotional, psychological, and spiritual. In this ever-changing, circular system, what we do on one level affects all levels. A breakdown at any level leads to illness because of the circular, related nature of homeostasis. When we do, feel, or think things that are not healthful for us, our balancing system will send messages to make changes in all aspects of our lives—health and lifestyle habits, relationships, profession, thinking patterns, feeling states, our living situation, and spiritual practices. The messages will come from a simple feeling of discomfort—or may scream at us in the form of pain, serious illness, accidents, and nightmares.

Think of it this way: look at the Ten of Wands from your tarot deck. It shows a person taking on too much, carrying a heavy burden. The journey looks painful, long, and slow. Now compare it to the Eight of Wands. Do you see the high energy and movement of the eight? It depicts regeneration and new ways forward. If we are holding a heavy load close to us and cannot release the burden (such as the Ten of Wands), we are unable to receive anything else. We get stuck in the same painful situation. Only by releasing the load can we receive the potent energy of healing, start over at a higher cycle, and move forward.

Another way to explain the cyclical stages of healing is to imagine a woman drowning in a pool. No attempt at rescue can help her because she is flailing her arms, afraid and fighting. She then makes a conscious choice to relax. The moment she decides to let go and stop fighting, she floats to the surface and is pulled from the water. The flow and process of healing is at once active and passive; releasing is a deliberate choice requiring action. Receiving something is passive—we allow it to happen. Recovery from dis-ease cannot be forced. By actively choosing to release our pain we allow ourselves to receive the gifts of healing.

Try a tarot layout called "Whatever Goes Around Comes Around" (refer to figure 9, p. 83). The outer circle (positions one–four) shows you what you need to actively release on the physical, emotional, psychological, and spiritual levels. The inner circle (positions five–eight) indicates what gifts you will receive in the healing process, using the same four levels. Spirituality comes from a place deep within, so I have placed the spiritual positions to the south, symbolized by fire and the creative, healing spark.

Please note: In this spread, the physical level can refer to your physical body, but it also depicts the everyday world and what you value: anything having to do with food, living arrangements, money, work/career, survival issues, nature, pets, and the senses, much like the suit of Pentacles.

You will read two cards together. For example, position two describes what you need to release on the emotional level. Position six shows the gift you will receive on the emotional level when you release position two. Position three describes what to release on the psychological level and position seven tells you the gift of healing you will receive when position three is released. And so it goes.

In other words, the inner circle of cards 5, 6, 7, and 8 are waiting for you when you make a conscious choice to release cards 1, 2, 3, and 4. Clear as mud, huh? Let's try it together because it's not as complicated as it appears. I'll use the cards that came up in my own reading as an example of how to interpret the spread. I was most concerned with my career. Indecision about my life work was literally making me sick. Please refer to chapter 8, as needed, but let your inner wisdom guide you.

As always, breathe deeply to achieve a state of relaxation. Speak aloud your intent to heal. Shuffle the cards and place them in positions one through eight as shown in figure 9. Turn the cards over and note your initial reaction to the spread. Look to see if there are any recurrent suits or numbers because repetition describes a theme or issue central to your healing. For example, if there are a lot of Swords, it describes painful decisions, psychological pain, the need to cut off from a painful past, or the need to make an important decision.

Let's say you have two or more Fives: what are you in conflict about? This conflict needs to be resolved for healing to occur. Several major arcana indicate issues of karma and spirituality and two or more court cards suggest that many people in your life are influencing you—for good or ill. It's up to you to decide how much to value the opinions of others.

Positions one and five are read together. Position one—what do I need to release on the physical level for healing to occur? What am I clinging to in the everyday world that impedes my progress? My position one card is the Two of Pentacles. A lot of my feelings of dis-ease revolve around my life work. I have been a registered nurse (R.N.) since 1977 and I have struggled with whether or not to let go of nursing in favor of writing. After all, nursing is practical and carries a regular paycheck. It's safe; a sure thing. Besides, I am competent and experienced. Despite this, writing, not nursing, feels like my life's work.

For several years I was on the fence about work and couldn't make a decision to save myself. I both dreaded and feared a change. The

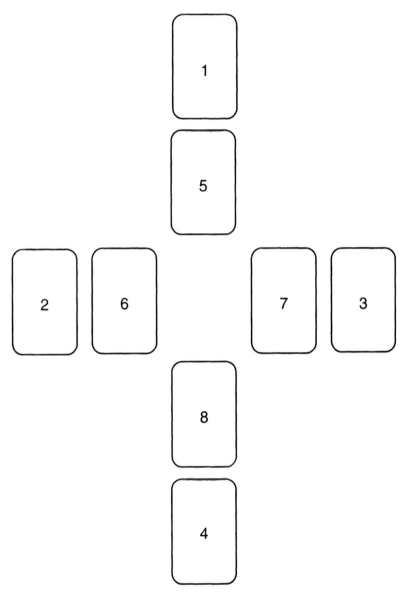

Figure 9*

Whatever Goes Around Comes Around

* *Key to figure 9:* Figure nine consists of two circles. *Outer circle* is positions one, two, three, and four (processing and releasing). *Inner circle* is positions five, six, seven, and eight (receiving and circulating). Please refer to text in chapter 5 for meanings of positions.

indecision contributed to stomach inflammation and depression. I was at a stalemate of indecision. My challenge was to get off the tight rope and make a decision about work, one way or the other.

Position five—what gift of healing will I receive on the physical level by releasing card 1? My position five card is the Ten of Pentacles, indicating financial security and the knowledge that what I value will also have lasting value to others. My legacy will not be in nursing and the Ten suggests my writing can have value to others long after I'm gone. By releasing indecision over work, I receive the gift of fulfillment, financial security, and lasting legacy.

Position two and six (taking position two first)—what do I need to release on the emotional level for healing to occur? I have the Seven of Cups, sometimes called the "fairy dust" card. I was emotionally attached to a lot of options about work. I could start my own tarot consultation service, go into private practice as an energetic healer, stay in traditional nursing, teach, try to write a book, or do any combination of the above. They all seemed like viable options and they all became subject to my fantasies and wishful thinking. Consequently, I made no decision and nothing got done.

Position six—what gifts of healing on the emotional level will I receive by releasing card 2? I received The World, suggesting that no decision was incorrect. I had spent so much time looking for just the right choice that it all became fantasy. By releasing my need to fantasize, I received the gift of growth and expansion. I stopped looking for the perfect decision and just made a decision to write, because the World told me all my options were good, as long as I did something. It was up to me to select one and get going. Yes, it was risky, but it was better than doing nothing at all.

Positions three and seven—position three first: what do I need to release on the psychological level for healing to occur? The Nine of Swords appeared and is often referred to as "the nightmare card." I had been agonizing about leaving the "acceptable" work as a nurse in a traditional setting. I come from a conservative family, proud to tell people I am an R.N., embarrassed to mention I am a tarot book author.

I wanted to do the right thing and not be an embarrassment to my family, yet I became angry with myself for being so dependent on my family of origin and their opinions. I am, after all, a middle-aged woman. Wasn't it about time to claim the real me and let the chips fall where they may? I feared horrible, vague repercussions from the decision to leave convention behind. I had nightmares about my family's rejection of me. I feared being ostracized from my family because of my interest in tarot.

Position seven—what gift of healing on the psychological level will I receive as a result of releasing card 3? I received The Hermit. It was an "ah-ha" experience. By going deep within to find my own source of wisdom, I could emerge as a light for others. The gifts of The Hermit are acceptance, patience, and understanding. By releasing my fear of rejection, I came to understand the natural order of things. I didn't need my family's approval to write about tarot. The Hermit told me to ask my own questions and take responsibility for my own beliefs. The promise of The Hermit is a patient acceptance of the consequences. I was asked to find an individual light where established religions had failed me. My unique spiritual climb had the potential to help others and I was on the right path.

Cards 4 and 8 are to be read together. Card 4—what do I need to release on the spiritual level for healing to occur? The Ten of Swords turned up, a card of absolute letting go. I had been clinging to old belief systems that were no longer useful to me and my need for familial approval was painful. I needed to look at my situation realistically. Yes, the Ten is a card of great loss, but by letting go of my old beliefs, I was promised the ability to get on with broader issues and growth. The Ten tells me to release past ideas and come to terms with what really is, not what I wanted or wished for. I might be able to receive family approval, but that was not my central issue. By letting go, I would be free to accomplish the things I was put here to do.

Position eight—what gift of healing on the spiritual level will I receive as a result of letting go of card 4? I received The Star, a card of hope and promise. The Star offers a sense of purpose and spiritual renewal. The

Star removes fear and asks what am I inspired to do? It told me that if I asked for help from the universe, I would receive it. By connecting to my inner wisdom, my life would have new meaning and purpose.

The Star also reminded me that life was not all or nothing/black or white thinking. I didn't have to choose between writing and my family. All I was required to do was be true to my inner guidance and the rest would take care of itself.

As I looked at the spread, I saw two Nines, two Tens, two Pentacles, and two Swords. I also had four major arcana out of an eight-card spread. All the pairs told me I needed to strive for balance in my life. My issues were of completion: Nines, leaving nursing; starting over at a higher cycle: Tens, writing; deciding what I valued: Pentacles, my life work; and the need to separate off from a painful past and make a decision: Swords, letting go of my need for approval. The four major arcana suggested that my choice of life work at this stage of development was a karmic or spiritual issue.

You can also read the spread across and perpendicular: Across are positions two, six, seven, and three—your emotional/mental expression of illness and health. Perpendicular (up and down) are positions one, five, eight, and four—your spiritual expression in everyday life. Reading the spread as a "cross" yields even more relationships in the spiral of dis-ease and healing.

Look for a conflict of suits. Think about how the elements of each suit interact with each other as you interpret this spread. For example, let's say you have Swords and Cups. What happens when air and water mix? Is it a devastating hurricane or comforting mist? For Pentacles and Wands, what happens when earth and fire mix? Are you warmed by it or does it cause a severe case of sunburn? Does air (Swords) feed fire (Wands) or blow it out? What do you get when Pentacles (earth) mix with Cups (water)? Are you in a mudslide or getting much-needed rain to end a drought?

Determining how the elements of suits interact with one another is one of the simplest, yet most revealing, methods of interpretation I have found. Make an entry in your journal. Can you see the circular, connected nature of healing?

Outcomes of healing

In modern medicine, healing is related to a return to function. If we have a broken leg, for example, the bones will heal and we will walk again. Functional return is part of the healing process, but there is more. In the broadest sense of the word, healing may not cure catastrophic diseases such as AIDS or cancer, but healing does restore an inner order to persons with serious illness. This restoration of balance fosters emotional strength, peace of mind, acceptance, and an inner knowing of wholeness.

If we consider healing to be an integration of physical, emotional, mental, and spiritual energies, then healing can take place whether or not there is a return to function. A person with AIDS may have a satisfying life and experience a pain-free and peaceful death. These experiences of integration and wholeness represent healing, even though the AIDS virus is still present. Yes, spontaneous remission of symptoms (curing) can and does occur, but healing is not the absence of disease—it's the presence of insight.

Healing energy always knows what is best for the one being healed—if we stay unattached to the end result. Developing the skill of nonattachment will greatly assist the process by allowing energy to flow naturally and find its greatest good for all. Healing takes place best when we let the energy come through us without a specific result in mind. All we need to do is visualize the perfection, or state of wholeness, within us.

Why?

Staying unattached to outcomes is ideal, but it doesn't stop the pain and confusion when we come face-to-face with unspeakable loss. I will be the first to tell you I have few answers to life's unanswerable questions.

My best friend died at the age of thirty-two, from a rare form of breast cancer, leaving two small boys without a mother. *No one* wanted to live more than she. My friend tried every known treatment, from radical surgery and chemotherapy to herbs and hands-on healing. Her catastrophic disease was not cured and it seemed so unfair to leave children, ages two and five, without a mother.

Did my best friend heal? I think so, but only she could have answered that with certainty. Were all of us who loved her too attached to the specific outcome of curing? Probably. I know she died peacefully in her sleep eight months after being diagnosed with cancer. My prayer is she died cradled in the loving arms of her creator.

I believe there are great and wise beings who watch over us, ready to pour their healing forces into us when we turn our attention to them. I also believe these same wise and compassionate beings are always near those who are ill and in pain, ready to bring comfort and ease distress. Sometimes, because we are human, we cannot comprehend the plan or soar high enough to see the overview—and we are left to wonder why.

Now that you understand healing and have contacted the healer within, chapter 6 offers activities and practical suggestions that support the healing process.

Notes to Chapter 5

1. Greer, Mary K. *Tarot for Your Self* (North Hollywood, California, Newcastle Publishing, 1984), p. 168.

Chapter 6

The Heart of Healing: Support for the Healing Process

Like an ability or muscle, hearing your inner wisdom is strengthened by doing it.

Robbie Gass

Different strokes for different folks

We all know of people who have sought traditional medical care with no relief, only to have a remission of symptoms with a nontraditional treatment such as acupressure or homeopathy. We also know a particular method can be successful with one person and fail miserably with another. Consider the fact two dissimilar methods of treatment can *both* be successful in treating the same ailment in certain individuals. Why do different methods work for different people?

I propose there is a common factor which influences success or failure and acts more deeply than the actual method of treatment used. I call it the *willingness* to heal. Put another way, it is the willingness to change and comes out of loving ourselves, not hating an illness. The process of healing is relieving obstructions on the physical, emotional, psychological, and spiritual levels—a process of letting go.

Healing is not dependent on any particular system of treatment such as homeopathy or allopathy (Western medicine). The criteria for choosing one treatment over another needs to be a simple one—does it work? *Any* treatment, traditional or nontraditional, will bring about the release of healing energy, provided we are willing to go deep within ourselves—and *accept whatever form the healing may take for our highest good.* For some, it will be a curing and return to function. For others, like my best friend, healing will result in a peaceful, pain-free death.

It is deceptive to believe that one—and only one—system of health care exceeds all others. A treatment isn't better because it's more mysterious, nor is it superior because it appears in *The New England Journal of Medicine.* All healing, whether by traditional or nontraditional means, occurs within us, working in cooperation with nature and perhaps the assistance of others.

Who can tell why a particular treatment works for one person and not another? We bring about the resolution of our own ailments, regardless of treatment choice. *Any* type of therapy that moves us closer to a state of wholeness is worthy of our attention. Whatever works, works. Without our cooperation, willingness to change and desire to get well, *all* methods of healing will fail.

Activities that support the healing process

Activities that support the healing process include, but are not limited to: centering, keeping a journal, meditating, spending time in nature, dream interpretation, and engaging in creative play. You've been centering, keeping a journal, and meditating throughout the exercises in *Tarot for the Healing Heart.* Let's look closer at creative play, spending time in the natural world and dream work.

Psychic play/sacred play

Healing is soul work and soul work is creating—and birthing—the life we want. Healing releases a surge of creative energy because we turn to the wisdom of our Higher Self and discover the healing creator within.

One way to connect to our inner resources is through creative self-expression. Since the goal is learning about the healing creator within, no artistic skill is needed. Use whatever medium is most suitable to express parts of yourself that might otherwise stay hidden. The secret to creative play is first centering—then remaining free of all judgmental or self-limiting thoughts.

Sing, dance, or just move to music; draw, paint, go to an art museum; read fairy tales and mythology; work with tarot, pendulums, runes, or the I-Ching; play a musical instrument, listen to music, compose a song; make jewelry; take photographs; read poetry or, better yet, write poetry; buy Play Doh and sculpt; finger paint, color with crayons, get messy. What are you naturally interested in? What did you enjoy as a child? Let your imagination soar.

The goal of creative play is to learn to trust your inner knowing. Without any particular intent other than self-discovery, you can recapture the joy and spontaneity you knew as a child. The more engaged the inner self becomes, the more the healer within will communicate with you—and the stronger your mind-body connection becomes.

Doing what comes naturally

Computers click, refrigerators hum, microwaves ding, cellular phones ring, TVs and radios blare. You can hear the blast of construction-site drills in the distance and a large truck just roared past your apartment window. Welcome to the modern era of noise.

We live in a fast-paced, technological society, and spend most of our lives in a mechanized culture. The more immersed we are in technology, the more regulated, clock-oriented, and analytical we become. By contrast, much of the healing process is natural, mysterious, and related to connecting with the universal life force. Aligning ourselves with the natural world can strengthen this connection. How can we, in the midst of life's busyness, find opportunities to spend time in the natural world? Our immersion in today's technological life dulls our sensitivity to the possible. External noise and busyness decrease our chances of hearing the inner voice of guidance. We narrow our perceptions of the possible.

By spending time in the natural world, we become part of the ebb and flow of nature and it becomes easier to understand the ebb and flow of illness and healing. When we become aware of natural rhythms, we have an opportunity to attune to the mysterious powers of healing. By observing the elements of weather in the wild, the beginning and end of natural days, the dark mystery of night, we can develop heightened sensitivity and respect for the cycle of life, death, and rebirth. Awareness of our connection to all living things (a glimpse of the higher overview), is one of the most important aspects of healing.

The seashore, jungle, desert, mountains, or deep forest are ideal, but you need not spend a lot of money to experience a place ruled by natural rhythms. Access to nature can be as close as your own backyard. Inexpensive ways to enhance your connection to Mother Earth include:

- Cultivate an herb or flower garden on your windowsill.
- Visit a park on a regular basis—lie on the grass and gaze at the sky.
- Go to a playground and ride the swing—feel fresh air on your face as you soar higher.
- Visit a zoo and pay close attention to the animals—better yet, volunteer at the zoo.
- Care for and cherish a pet—observe your pet's natural cycles of rest and activity.
- Take an early morning walk as the sun rises.
- Take late night walks under starry skies (and remember to choose an area where you feel safe).
- Walk barefoot on grass.
- Walk in the snow, build a snowman, or make snow angels.
- Make a pile of autumn leaves—then jump in them.
- Care for growing potted plants in your work and living areas.
- Photograph a tree every month for a year, then make a scrapbook with your pictures, showing the beauty of changing seasons.
- Make ongoing journal notes about the colors, smells, characteristics, and feelings of whatever season you are currently experiencing.

- Read the poetry of Robert Louis Stevenson: "Sing a song of seasons / Something bright in all / Flowers in the summer / Fires in the fall."

- If your area has an arboretum, observatory, or planetarium, visit them all and connect to earth, moon, and sky.

- Become an amateur astronomer—buy a beginners guide to the galaxy, cover a flashlight with red cellophane (or purchase a child's telescope for $20.00), and start gazing at the stars—in all the different seasons.

- Pitch a tent and camp out in your own back yard—spend the evening star-gazing or listening to the natural sounds of night .

- Walk in the rain (avoid walking in thunderstorms because of lightning).

- Listen to a thunderstorm and make a journal entry about the power of nature.

- Collect stones and build an outdoor cooking pit—then use it (check local fire safety regulations first).

- Look for objects from nature and arrange an indoor altar or centerpiece (mine includes feathers, shells, pine cones, beautiful or unusual rocks, and crimson leaves).

- Maintain a birdfeeder (out of kitty's reach, of course) and enjoy the beauty of your feathered friends.

- Keep a fish tank and let the tranquility of water soothe your soul.

- Take work breaks outside whenever possible, to refresh your spirit.

- Do anything else that intuitively occurs to you, based on the uniqueness of your particular geographic area (and always remember personal safety).

When we master the art of quieting the mind by centering and attuning to the natural world, we are able to release or transform burdensome care and concerns. We increase our sensitivity to the ebb and flow of life and it is this sensitivity that further enables us to understand and express the healing process.

By increasing our awareness of nature, we experience the fact we are not separate beings, but all related to a greater whole. In nature, we learn there is no randomness. When we give thanks for these fresh insights, we acknowledge our place in the universe and open up to dimensions beyond the physical realm.

Perchance to dream: keeping a dream journal

Reread "The Healing Power of Dreams" section found in the introduction. The technique of dream recording is at once simple and difficult. Recording a dream *the minute you wake up* is the last thing most of us want to do immediately upon waking, but if dreams are not written down at once, they fade away like mist under the morning sun.

When you give your dream a name such as "The Beach" try to associate tarot card symbolism with it. What card does "The Beach" remind you of? The Queen of Cups, perhaps, or The Moon? Just like tarot, dreams are a medium for the expression of symbolism. A dream can clarify how a particular tarot card relates to your life or give you new ideas about the message it's trying to convey.

The insights you gain from a tarot reading may be expanded upon in your dreams. You can ask your higher self for a dream that gives more information about how a card is expressed in your life or how its energies affect you. The trick to incubating a tarot dream is thorough preparation before you settle in for that long winter's nap: studying the card's picture in detail so that you can close your eyes and vividly recall its details, meditating with it, reading what others say about it.

Immerse yourself in every possible aspect of the card. On the night you want to "dream tarot," write your request on a piece of paper: How does The Moon express itself in my life? Or: What do I need to know about the Queen of Cups and the healing process? Place the request and the card in question underneath your pillow. As you drift off to sleep, say aloud, "Tonight I will remember my dreams."

In the morning record your dream in as much detail as possible. Don't worry if the associations are not immediately clear. Repeat the procedure for the next two or three nights. It may take several days before the message becomes clear.

Although some of the images in your dream may be identical to a card, much of the time they will not be. Most likely, the dream will include your own symbolism that elaborates on the card's meaning. For example, you ask for a dream about The Moon. That night you dream about a cat and wake up wondering what on earth happened. You discover, over time, that your own symbol for intuition and inner wisdom is a cat—the positive, creative aspect of the feminine. The message of how to use The Moon in the healing process, then, is to engage in activities that develop your psychic/sacred self.

Dreams and dream work are extensive topics. Browse a bookstore, but remember, the dream belongs to the dreamer. It is ultimately up to you to decide the truest meaning of a dream. Don't fall into the trap of supposing that this or that theorist has the whole truth. Take—from anyone—whatever makes sense to you. If you feel an approach does not go far enough, move on to another one. My all-time favorite dream book is Joan Mazza's *Dreaming Your Real Self: A Personal Approach to Dream Interpretation* (Berkeley Publishing Group, 1998), but go wherever you feel called.

One last note: A book will tell you what interpretation you might give your dreams. Your dreams will tell you what interpretation you should be giving them. If a fox appears in your dream, remember that Mother Nature didn't put a goose or zebra there. Decide what the symbolism of the *fox* is for you—and happy dreaming.

Psychic development and playing with the tarot

For a lot of folks, the word "psychic" has a bad reputation because it conjures visions of 1-900 hotlines. For reasons beyond me, I often see the word "psychic" accompanied by an exclamation point: "Psychic Readings! Let a psychic tell you your future! First two minutes of psychic phone consultation free!" In many areas, being psychic is considered a joke, a scam, only for the chosen few, evil— or just plain weird.

The negative connotation surrounding the word "psychic" is unfortunate because the word comes from the Greek word *psukhe*, meaning "soul."[1] Psychic development is soul development, and soul development is the essence of the healing process: understanding that our true nature is spiritual and the physical body is an instrument of divine expression. There is nothing unnatural about being psychic—in fact, hearing the voice of the soul is the most natural state of all.

Many wonderful books are available about psychic development. My favorite is *The Psychic Pathway: A Workbook for Reawakening the Voice of Your Soul* by Sonia Choquette (Crown Trade Paperbacks, 1995). Don't take my word for it—go to a bookstore and let your inner wisdom guide you.

Methods of developing psychic ability include creating mandalas, working with a pendulum or runes, studying the Kabbala or I Ching—and of course, playing with the tarot. We examined tarot as therapy in chapter 4. Used as therapy, tarot emphasizes emotional and psychological healing. Let's look at tarot as creative play for psychic/soul development.

On a very basic level, playing with tarot stimulates right-brain activity, and right-brain competence encourages psychic/soul development. I like to think of tarot play as sacred play, that is, playing with a purpose: moving into a loving awareness of ourselves and our world, finding creativity, serenity, laughter, and empowerment.

Tarot symbols are strong. They work especially well for people who are visually oriented, who can imagine in pictures and can see images in their mind's eye when they meditate. If you don't naturally see images in your imagination, you may not be drawn to tarot cards. But, if you want to *develop* your "third eye" (sixth chakra) and improve your psychic imagery skills, cards are a great method. Relax and don't try to force it.

It's all in the cards

The following suggestions are ways to psychically play with tarot cards. Use the ideas to ignite your own playful imagination—and *have fun:*

- Photocopy your tarot cards: Enlarge the cards and then color them yourself, without looking at the original deck. For example, what color is The High Priestess in your mind's eye? (And no fair peeking at your cards.)

• Use the cards to develop psychometry. Psychometry is the ability to receive information by holding a related object. Place your cards face-down and select one without turning it over. Hold it in your receptive hand. (If you're right-handed, your receptive hand is probably the left one. Vice versa for lefties like me.) Let your mind relax and receive impressions about the card you are holding. Turn it over and compare your impressions with the actual card. Did you see colors, shapes, get "a feeling" or an idea? Did your impressions match the actual card? For instance, if you held a Wand, what color or feeling did you receive? Red or orange? Warm?

• Choose a tarot card to accompany you through the day: Think about the card as you make choices and decisions. What would The Magician or Queen of Cups do today? What would they have for lunch? What color clothing would they wear? How would they respond to each situation you find yourself in today?

• Practice telling stories: A tarot reading involves the ability to weave together different characters. Find a child and ask her if you can tell a story. Start with one you know, then add to it. Pull a tarot card and start a story. When you are out of ideas, select another card and continue with the same story. Pull as many cards as needed to make a flowing tale. Be sure to include plot, character, setting, and central theme.

• Choose a card a day and write down everything that comes to mind about that card, just by looking at the picture. Do not refer to a book of definitions. Then compare your impressions with the traditional meanings found in any basic tarot book.

• Separate your cards into piles of positive, negative, and neutral categories. Why do certain cards repel or attract you?

• Choose a Minor or Major Arcana card and write a story, poem, or song about it.

• Write a story, poem, or song about a court card.

• Buy a blank deck and draw your own tarot cards. Be sure to color them.

- Think of people in the news and decide what tarot card best represents them. For example, what card symbolizes the U.S. president?

- Throw an imaginary party and invite characters from the tarot deck. How would these characters interact with one another?

- Incubate a dream using a tarot card: ask the card for specific information, place the card under your pillow, and whisper that you will remember the dream when you wake up. Record *any* impressions as soon as you awaken. If it's unclear, ask the card again on another night. Be patient. Answers will come.

- My personal favorite: gently pile tarot cards face-down on your favorite sleeping pet or best-loved human. (Yes, they will question your sanity— or at least, stare indignantly.) When your pet or human wakes up or moves, read any cards that have fallen off face-up. These cards will give you clues about your relationship with your loved one for the day—furry or otherwise. And remember, this is psychic play. Have fun.

Your own wise counsel: a meditation with the King or Queen of Cups

For good or ill, we need a modicum of emotional maturity to prosper in this life. The healing process requires us to loosen our hold on rigid thinking patterns and let go of worn-out ideas requires emotional maturity. But, what in the world is emotional maturity and, better yet, how do you develop it? We don't just wake up one morning and say, "OK, today I am emotionally mature."

The following meditation will help you determine where you are emotionally strong and where you need to focus your efforts for change. I call it "Your Own Wise Counsel." The King and Queen of Cups are the emotional counselors of the tarot.

The Queen has a depth of emotion that makes feelings central to her existence. She has a fullness of expression and understanding that nurtures others. She is the soul mediating between spirit and daily life, and she has learned to trust her intuition. She takes her emotional understanding into herself and applies it to the everyday world.

The King is more of an outer-directed emotional authority. He has tremendous humor about life's predicaments. His feelings are under control, but with a detached awareness. He is the wounded healer—he heals himself by healing others.

His worldly wisdom comes from painful experiences that are deeply truthful. He has had to work at being united with his feelings because this union does not come easily for the King. He takes his emotional understanding and directs it outward to help others.

Decide which type of emotional understanding attracts you most. If you were selecting a counselor, would you better relate to the Queen or King of Cups? Pull either the King or Queen from your tarot deck. If you can't decide, use them both. Gaze at the King or Queen of Cups and ask your own wise counselor the following questions:

1. What emotions are currently active in my life?

2. How do I deal with negative or painful emotions?

3. In what ways am I a caregiver or counselor?

4. How do I nurture myself?

5. Is emotional support needed at this time?

Don't rush this meditation. Make an initial entry in your healing journal and add insights as they occur to you over time. It takes tremendous courage to ask for help—a lion's heart. You are dealing with wounds, not defects. Determine where you are emotionally strong and where you need to concentrate your efforts for change—then take loving action on your own behalf and get help if you need it.

Choices, choices

The best time to choose a health practitioner is when you are in good health. You will have time to make a careful choice. Unfortunately, in the era of health maintenance organizations (HMOs), choosing a medical doctor depends more on your insurance policy that it does on personal preference.

Complementary health practitioners offer more freedom of choice because they are usually not members of HMOs. The upside to this is you are free to choose. The downside is all payment for a service rendered comes out of your own pocket, but check your insurance policy—many services once considered "alternative" are now part of standard insurance coverage.

Ask your friends and neighbors for a recommendation. Once you have a name, contact the practitioner's office and ask for references, which will tell you more about the person's qualifications. Make sure the practitioner is appropriately qualified to your own satisfaction.

Stop right there—if getting the name of a reputable practitioner seems like an impossible task, then choosing a specific type of treatment can feel like an unanswerable riddle. OK, you've been having symptoms, you've done an exercise or two in this book, and you've decided to seek treatment.

Now you must decide what *type* of therapy best suits your needs. The choices can make you dizzy. It is not within the scope of this book to describe all known complementary therapies. Look in the Yellow Pages, make phone calls, search the web, go to the public library, call any hospital that offers a "whole life" (alternative therapy) department, browse the health section of a bookstore— and become *informed* about the options available to you.

Physician/Healer

Tarot can help you decide on the most appropriate treatment for your situation. Any time we face several options, we can choose a card for each choice to see what they might offer us. We should never base important decisions only on the cards, but they can help us consider the issues and make our important decisions a little easier.

Try a spread I call "Physician, Healer" to shed some light on your treatment conundrums. It is important to research two to four types of therapies before you begin. Get enough information, at least, to understand what each treatment might have to offer you, according to your specific health concern. I'll use my own layout as an example.

At the top of a journal page, list the two to four treatment options you are considering. I was having painful problems with my stomach (again) after being diagnosed two years earlier with a gastric ulcer. I did a little research and decided upon medical doctor, healing touch practitioner, and herbal remedies as my three most likely choices.

Next, shuffle the deck and randomly lay a tarot card next to each treatment choice. My "Physician/Healer" spread looked like this:

Medical doctor—Page of Swords

Healing touch—Four of Swords

Herbal remedy—Queen of Pentacles

The Page of Swords told me that seeking a medical doctor's care would involve painful, "knife-like" invasive tests, or perhaps surgery. The Four of Swords suggested that I needed to rest and healing touch would help me do that. It also told me that the integrative experience of unblocking and balancing my energy fields might bring some painful psychological issues to the surface. The Queen of Pentacles reminded me that I needed to nurture myself and pay attention to my body. It suggested that an herbal treatment would nurture me from the inside out by using a gift or two from Mother Earth.

In the end, I chose healing touch and herbal remedies. The stomach discomfort dissipated. True to the cards, painful psychological issues came to the surface during my healing touch sessions. I began seeing a counselor and *Tarot for the Healing Heart* was born.

A card for each treatment option will help you look at the different qualities each offers. You may be able to imagine how your body will respond to a specific remedy. Notice in my layout that the cards do not choose one course of action over another. Instead, Physician/Healer will help you see what might happen in any given situation. Compare the images on the cards to your own inner sense of what's right for you.

A tarot reading often helps acknowledge what you already know. This layout will give you a snapshot, or summary, of the situation and the choices available to you. Before and after the first visit, ask yourself the following questions:

- Are you comfortable with the practitioner's age and gender?

- Do you have easy access to the office? How far do you have to travel?

- Is the office clean and the staff courteous?

- Can you reach the practitioner to schedule an appointment without much delay?

- Did you have to wait long to see the practitioner?

- Did the provider put you at ease, listening to your concerns and answering any questions you had?

- If you were given a test or asked to buy a treatment, medicine, or herb, did you understand what it was for, how much it cost, how to use it correctly, and what to do if you had problems?

- Determine you need a second opinion if: your practitioner recommends anything that feels radical to you, a rare or fatal condition is diagnosed, your practitioner does not seem to know what to do for you, or your symptoms don't improve over time.

- Did you feel satisfied with your first visit—and, most importantly—did you sense yourself to be a partner in your own health care decisions?

Make sure you describe exactly what the problem is at the first appointment and tell your new practitioner if you are under the care of another health professional or taking any prescribed medications. Don't expect your practitioner to guess or divine your symptoms. Ask questions and impart details. Make a note of the things you'd like to discuss on the first visit and don't be afraid to refer to your notes. If you don't think your practitioner listens to you or communicates clearly enough, tell him or her so. If things don't improve, consider changing practitioners. It's your money, your body, your health, and your life.

Know when to say when

Tarot is a wonderful tool to unlock intuition, establish the mind-body connection, and engage the unconscious in the healing process, but working with tarot is not a cure-all or panacea. New insights from tarot will sometimes alert you to the fact you need outside assistance to engage the healer within. Put simply, know when to say when. The type of treatment you seek is your choice based on your life experience. Call a medical doctor or healing practitioner if:[2]

- There is an unusual discharge or bleeding.
- For women, there's been a marked change in menstruation cycle (pain, decrease or increase in flow).
- A sore doesn't heal in three weeks.
- A lump appears in your breast.
- You have chronic indigestion, difficulty swallowing, recurrent vomiting; there is a marked change in your bowel and bladder habits, including difficulty with urine stream.
- You have blurred vision or see a halo around lights; you have unexplained faintness or dizziness.
- You have severe shortness of breath; or your lips, eyelids, or nails have a bluish tint.
- You experience a sudden loss of weight or appetite; or you have excessive thirst.
- You have a nagging cough or hoarseness; or a fever above 103 degrees Fahrenheit.
- A mole, freckle, or blemish changes color.
- You have unusual weakness or fatigue; or there is a yellowing of your skin or eyes.
- Your ankles are severely swollen or you have pain in the calves of either leg, especially accompanied by pain on flexion (pointing your toes towards the ceiling).
- There is unexplained severe pain, especially in the head, chest, or abdomen.
- You simply don't feel well, and not feeling well has interfered with your activities of daily living.

Breaking the pain cycle

No other physical experience is as heavily embued with meaning as pain. The idea that pain is simply the result of an internal condition is recent. We need look no further than *Dante's Inferno*, *Paradise Lost*, or the Christian Bible to find pain and suffering from external sources.

How we experience pain depends on our personal belief systems. Pain is a subjective experience. The experience of pain cannot be reduced to mere physiology any more than it can be neatly explained by social or moral standards. The difficulty in understanding pain stems from its complicated origin in both realms—as a function of our bodies and a statement of our cultural identities.

Understanding your own multifaceted experience of pain becomes important in learning to break the pain cycle. Ask yourself: what does the experience of pain mean *to me*? Make a journal entry about your personal definition of pain. Write the word "pain" across the top of the page and free-associate for a few minutes.

Traditional forms of treatment, such as use of pain medicine* or physical therapy, can work well with alternative approaches to pain control such as acupuncture, hypnosis, or biofeedback. Pain management doesn't have to be an either/or proposition. Experiment with different methods until you find a combination that relieves your pain. Whatever works, works.

Going within to stop pain: a meditation with The Hermit

Pull The Hermit, No. 9, from your tarot deck. The Hermit gently urges us to go within ourselves to find our solutions. The Hermit represents illumination of the inner world when the outer one is dark. He teaches us the need for solitude to find our inner strength. He provides comfort and warmth despite the gloom, and reminds us that we are more than our physical bodies.

---

* Do not be afraid to take pain medicine if you need it, but avoid combining it with alcohol. Pharmacology has its place. People do not become addicted to analgesics taken as prescribed for genuine pain.

In order to reduce pain, The Hermit asks you to remember that *you are not your pain*. He understands the natural rhythms of life and urges you to realize that the cycle of health and illness waxes and wanes—even the intensity of pain varies from moment to moment. The Hermit helps you accept where you are at any given juncture and gently whispers, "This, too, shall pass."

Place The Hermit on the healing altar where you can see it without straining your eyes. Begin by creating an atmosphere of healing as described throughout the book.

Become aware of your breathing. As you breathe in, raise your shoulders to your ears without tightening the neck. Gently hold the tension for a moment. Now relax and exhale, allowing the shoulders to drop. Do this a few more times until you feel relaxed. Be slow and gentle throughout the meditation.

Next, as you inhale and raise your shoulders, locate the pain—the reason you are doing this exercise. With your shoulders raised, say, "At this moment I feel pain." Upon exhalation and lowering your shoulders, say, "At this moment I feel relaxed." Remember to do this without tightening your neck. You are now ready to go within to break the pain cycle.

Look at the image of The Hermit. Upon exhalation, imagine all your pain flowing out of your feet into the earth, leaving empty space where it once was in your body. Breathe in white light and let it flow to fill the area where your pain was. Feel the space permeating with a loving white light.

Allow the edges of the card to blur slightly and step inside to be with the gentle Hermit. Now when you exhale, let your pain flow from you to The Hermit. Your pain flows out his feet to the solid earth he is standing on. The painful energy that is draining off is neutral and does not have a positive or negative quality outside your body. It quickly dissipates into Mother Earth.

The Hermit holds his lantern above your head. You feel warm, safe, and protected. Breathe in the beautiful lantern light from above. It fills the empty space where your pain was and radiates throughout your body. You are at peace and relaxed. The Hermit whispers advice about ways to go within to stop pain. What does he tell you? The pain is gone. Now you fully understand the natural ebb and flow of life, including the waxing and waning of pain.

Stay in the warmth of The Hermit's light for as long as you like. Slowly step out of the image of The Hermit and allow the card to be two-dimensional once more. Return to the room and gently open your eyes. Breathe deeply, look around. Place your hands on the chair or floor to ground energy. Wiggle your toes. You are not your pain. Make an entry in your journal about going within to stop pain. What did you learn from the wise, gentle Hermit?

The compulsion to repeat

I am a slow learner. I don't know about you, but I have to make the same mistake several times before I finally hear the message. One of the most troubling realizations to make about our humanness is that things go wrong over and over again in the same way. Sound familiar? I call it the compulsion to repeat: the unbearable feeling of being stuck, the mental equivalent of wading through molasses.

Having once caught a glimpse of this tendency, it is impossible to forget. Attempts to resolve it by ourselves are rarely successful. There is always more to the story than we are consciously aware of and this can't be brought into view without someone else's help.

Almost always, the compulsion to repeat behavior that harms our health comes from the past. For example, in a crowd of strangers, the one individual with no personal boundaries will invariably meet the one neediest person in the room—a natural match. Unconsciously, we reenact the disturbed relationships from our childhood and unwittingly pick out individuals from around us who will—for similar reasons of their own—be compelled to join in. Patterns are repeated until we hear the message.

Wounds from the past—and the compulsion to repeat the wounding—can cause overwhelming pain, suffering, and illness. Asking for help when you need it is an act of courage and sign of strength. Whatever works, works. If you need help with the compulsion to repeat, get it. Don't hold yourself back from healing.

Some of the most common reasons for professional counseling are eating disorders, sexual abuse, rape, alcohol and substance abuse, bereavement, being haunted by the past (post-traumatic stress disorder), depression, anxiety, relationship problems and a general dissatisfaction with life.[3] This is not an all-inclusive list. Wounds come in a variety of shapes and sizes. Check your local yellow pages for services in your area or search the web for information.

My favorite website for health information is "Health A to Z: a comprehensive site," everything from anxiety disorders to zinc dosages. It has both traditional and nontraditional information (listed under "Alternative Medicine"). Health A to Z is easy to use—just click and go, and it has many links. The site is for nonmedical people and the cyberspace-challenged among us. *Address:* http://www.healthatoz.com

When Spider Webs Unite

When spider webs unite, they scare away the lions.
Hindu proverb

There is strength in numbers. Groups are sprouting up everywhere in astonishing variety: women's spirituality (commonly called sacred circles), consciousness-raising, support, self-help, therapy, twelve-step; you name it, there's a group for it. But what about starting a group in your own home?

A sacred circle is not just a meeting with the chairs rearranged. A circle is a way of doing things differently than we have been accustomed to—listening without an agenda, rotating leadership—a chance to speak plainly and be intimately known based on honesty, equality, and spiritual integrity.

It is important to distinguish between a spirituality group and a therapy or support group because the lines between them sometimes blur. Therapy and recovery groups are problem oriented. Support groups focus on painful pasts and obstacles for growth. People come to support groups to heal. Spirituality groups are intensely personal, but they don't dwell on individual problems; instead, the group explores, expresses, and develops its own experience and understanding of spirituality.[4]

If you think that you would like to form a support group for healing or a spirituality group for understanding, I recommend two books: *Sacred Circles: A Guide to Starting Your Own Women's Spirituality Group* by Robin Deen Carnes and Sally Craig (HarperCollins, 1996); and *Calling the Circle: The First and Future Culture* by Christina Baldwin (Bantam Books, 1998).

Both books present detailed instructions for getting started, sharing goals, and solving disagreements. Baldwin's book can used for any group process, including spirituality and support, while *Sacred Circles* focuses exclusively on women's spirituality.

Creating an atmosphere of intention, respect, and openness is no small task. In fact, in can be downright overwhelming. If you'd like to form a group in your own home, why not think of your group in terms of tarot? I call the following checklist "When Spider Webs Unite":

The Suit of Wands: Creating the group with passion. How will you get started? What planning is needed? What group activities do you imagine? How will anger be resolved?

The Suit of Cups: Put your heart into it. What kind of commitment to the group are you willing to make? Will your group include emotional, psychic, or women's issues? Will you discuss dreams and relationships?

The Suit of Swords: Communication, ideas, and conflict. What will the agenda be? How will conflict within the group be resolved? How will you evaluate the group's progress? How will you brainstorm for topics?

The Suit of Pentacles: Building your group on solid ground, practical matters, manifesting, staying power, hands-on activities, food and refreshments, support. What is the foundation of the group? How will practical matters such as meeting time, place, frequency, and refreshments be established? What type of hands-on activities will support the group process?

The Court Cards: The personality of the group. Will there be shared leadership? What will be the actual personality (focus) of the group? Will the group have a name to explain its focus and personality?

The Major Arcana: Connecting to the sacredness of the group. How will new members be introduced to the group? What is the therapeutic or spiritual value of the group? Will you have ritual? Will you honor rites of passage? In what ways can you let go with closure and dignity when it's time to disband?

Starting and maintaining a group—for healing, support, or spirituality—is challenging, rewarding, and fun. Good luck—may your spider webs unite and scare away all lions.

The heart of healing

There really is strength in numbers and we do not have to be alone. The heart of healing is locating the right kind of support for your own healing process. The last tarot layout in the "heart series" is called "The Heart of Healing," to assist you in finding your correct path to healing. Its purpose is to help you evaluate your healing awareness—the progress you've made, the tools you have, where you are strong, and what work still needs to be done.

Begin with deep breathing to achieve a feeling of relaxation. Shuffle the cards and deal them face-down in positions one through five as shown in figure 10. If you don't understand a specific position, simply shuffle the deck and draw another card for advice or more information.

Position One—The Heart of Healing: What must I support and nurture in order to heal? What is the essence of my healing process?

Position Two—Awareness: Tools to Work with Today: What am I aware of now that I wasn't before? What tools for healing do I have available to me right now?

Position Three—Blocks: Work to be Done: What do I need to bring into consciousness so I can heal? What blocks do I have that could sabotage the healing process?

Position Four—Strengths and Lessons Learned: What strengths do I have that will support the healing process? What lessons have I learned from the message of dis-ease?

Position Five—Advice: Action to be Taken and Future Direction: What concrete action can I take in my own behalf to support the healing process?
What advice does this card give me about my future direction?

Make an entry in the journal about your own creative process of
healing.

Déjà vu: contemplating the cards

By keeping a tarot journal, you may start to notice repeating cards or repeating
suits: Oh, drats, there's that pesky Hanged Man again. If you review your readings, you may discover suits that predominate: Why do I always get Swords? You
may also be curious about why certain suits or cards never appear: My friend
always gets the Ten of Cups, why can't I?

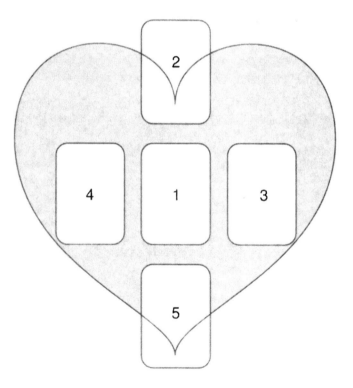

Figure 10
The Heart of Healing

By reviewing your readings, you can get an overview of the issues in your life. With periodic overviews of past readings, patterns will start to emerge. Ask yourself what themes keep appearing. Ask yourself, too, what themes never seem to show up.

For example, if you have money worries and there's not a Pentacle in sight (but lots of Cups), why might this be so? Could it be that money is more of an emotionally charged issue than a question of actual financial security?

In my own experience as a professional consultant, I question the seeker when a relationship spread is on the table and no Cups appear. Does that mean love is not an issue or does it hint that my client's heart isn't in the relationship? I have also found that a financially stable seeker will rarely have a Pentacle in the spread, unless it's the Nine.

In other words, cards and suits that never appear mean one of two things: (1) it's not an issue, or, (2) it's an issue that is being blocked or avoided. With a little contemplation, you will be able to decide which it is for you.

If you notice repeating cards, try an exercise I call "Déjà vu." For repeating suits, ask these questions:

Wands—What can I do? What action should I take? What fires me up?

Cups—What am I feeling? What am I dreaming? What does my intuition say?

Swords—What decision needs to be made? What am I thinking (or worrying) about? Where is my pain?

Pentacles—What do I value? What is my body trying to tell me? What are my instincts trying to tell me?

For repeating Court Cards, ask:

What is my stage of development? What is my persona in certain situations? Who is influential or important to me? How do the people in my life affect me?

For repeating Major Arcana cards, ask:

What qualities need to be expressed? What is being tested? How am I dealing with a situation? What is my Karma? Where are my strengths? How do I need to grow? How can I express my capacity to heal?

Select one of the questions from the above list that has particular interest to you now. Close your eyes and reflect on the question. What images, feelings, or words come to mind? Do you notice any physical sensations? Write an uncensored response in your journal. This contemplative activity offers a fresh perspective—looking at tarot from a different angle. Studied over time, the answers may surprise you with their clarity.

Working your way through

When we are ill or injured we may be flooded with emotion, especially at first. Gradually the hurt is diminished and we adapt to any necessary changes, but real healing comes from the work we do in the recovery process. We become stronger, wiser—and empowered—to find meaning in our lives based on our wounding.

I do not ascribe to fluffy, bluebird-of-happiness advice. Pain hurts, and venting powerful emotions in a constructive manner is critical to recovery. Based on my own wounding and recovery, I have developed some hints for healing. I hope you find them useful:

- Give time time—Patience with your own healing process is more than a virtue, it's a necessity. The clenched fist of impatience only aggravates the pain cycle.

- What is buried alive stays alive—Voicing your anger, resentment, and fear accelerates the healing process because it is truthful. The worst thing you can do when you are ill is buck up and bury powerful emotions that can kill you.

- Wallow—Give yourself twenty minutes a day to feel sorry for yourself, as well as depressed, angry, and resentful; then let it go and do something constructive (like reading *Tarot for the Healing Heart*).

- Whatever works, works—Get professional guidance if you need it. A therapist can help you with the real feelings of fear, loss, anger, and resentment. She or he can also suggest constructive ways for you to actively help yourself.

- Find someone you can trust—a spiritual adviser or friend—someone who can emotionally support you as you move through the pain and regain a sense of hope.

Take Heart

In the country of the blind, the one-eyed man is king.
Michael Apostoluis

Over time, I have learned that gifts come in strange packages. It is said that necessity is the mother of invention. I believe the human spirit is strong. We can accomplish almost anything we want, no matter what the obstacles, given the time, desire—or necessity—to do so. As the author George Eliot said, "It is never too late to be what you might have been." May your inner journey be filled with light and love.

Notes to Chapter 6

1. *The American Heritage Dictionary.* Margery S. Berube, Director of Editorial Operations (Boston, Houghton Mifflin Company, 1982), p. 999.

2. *Mosby's Conventional Medicine/Alternative Medicine: Choices of Treatment for Your Most Common Medical Problems.* Caroline Green, Editor (St. Louis, Mosby-Year Book, Inc., 1998), p. 6.

3. Avery, Brice. *Thorsons Principles of Psychotherapy* (San Francisco, Thorsons, an imprint of HarperCollins Publishers, 1996), p. 16.

4. Carnes, Robin Deen and Sally Craig. *Sacred Circles: A Guide to Creating Your Own Women's Spirituality Group* (New York, HarperCollins, 1998), p. 3.

PART FOUR

WHOLE NEW WORLD

*Be a Columbus to whole new continents and worlds within
you, opening new channels, not of trade, but of thought.*

Henry David Thoreau

Chapter 7

HORIZONS

There is a test to find if your mission on earth is finished.
If you're alive, it isn't.

Richard Bach

~∞~

The wounded healer

You may want to try the healing techniques found in this book on your friends and loved ones. In our sincere, but often misguided, efforts to be of service, we rush headlong into healing others before we ourselves are healed. We evolve as healers when we participate in *our own healing* first through attunement to our inner wisdom. As we move closer to higher consciousness, we become involved with healing and the growth process at all levels: physical, emotional, psychological, and spiritual.

A primary way we can develop into healers (and be of service to others) is to have firsthand experience with healing our own pain. At some point, we must examine our own wounds, look at our weaknesses, and recognize and develop our own strengths.

It is only when we face and integrate the messages of our dis-ease that we allow a powerful healing dimension to be born. Without healing ourselves, or channeling our wounds into healing conduits, there is little chance of emerging with the strength to heal others.

Tarot is a mirror to your soul and a reflection of you. The unintentional projection of your personal pain can occur while reading tarot for others. Use caution when reading the cards for another: be aware of your own issues and prejudices. Don't fall into the trap of "inflicting" a tarot reading onto others.

As you address your own woundedness, remember that the most powerful healing technique you can use to heal people close to you is to determine what they reflect in you, then heal that issue in yourself.

Self-healing is a lifelong process. Just because we emerge healed from one crisis doesn't mean we have completed our soul work. As long as we live, we will continue to have unexpected challenges and opportunities to develop wisdom. It is through our ongoing conscious awareness of personal pain—and courageous acts of self-healing—that we learn compassion, forgiveness, and love to emerge with the qualities of a healer.

Tarot and . . .

The one quality complementary therapies have in common is the strengthening of the mind-body connection. Throughout this book I have proposed that healing is to make whole. I believe a tarot reading can be an act of healing because it has the potential to increase our awareness of the overall patterns and energies of our lives.

The highly symbolic tarot images can be a powerful aid to the creative, healing imagination. In her wonderful book *The Tarot: Methods, Mastery and More*, Cynthia Giles suggests that the tarot will one day be used with expressive arts therapy—combining tarot with music, art, dance, writing, and drama to assist the healing process.[1]

Because scents affect the emotional centers of the brain and emotions have a powerful effect on immunity, aromatherapy is an enjoyable aid to wellness. The power of scent is strong and closely related to imagination. One of the lasting childhood memories I have of my father is picking apples with him on our large farm during the crisp, golden afternoons of autumn. To this day, the smell of apples reminds me of that happy time.

What are your memories of smell? What do you feel when you recall the aroma of fresh-baked bread? Because smell evokes such powerful memories, combining tarot and aromatherapy can be used for healing in readings, meditation, and ritual.

The Essence of Magic by Mary K. Greer (Newcastle Publishing, 1993) eloquently covers the topic of aromatherapy and tarot for healing. Unfortunately, this book is out of print, but well worth the effort of a book search. If you are lucky enough to locate a copy, cherish it, because *The Essence of Magic* is a treasure.

You can even use tarot to create herbal therapies and understand how plants are healers of mind, body, and spirit. *The Spirit of Herbs* and its accompanying deck, *The Herbal Tarot,* by Michael Tierra and Candis Cantin, offer thorough explanations of various herbs; as well as the symbolic connections to tarot. If you are interested in herbal remedies and tarot, consult *The Spirit of Herbs and Herbal Tarot* deck for guidance (U.S. Games, Inc., 1993).

Are you attracted to the idea of "spider webs uniting"? If you feel there is strength in numbers and like group support with ritual, then Vicki Noble's book is for you. *Making Ritual with Motherpeace Cards* (Three Rivers Press, 1998) will show you how to use the imagery of tarot cards to align yourself with the larger forces of the universe. She offers beautiful ritual ideas in the group setting and advice on healing with tarot.

This is by no means an exhaustive list of the creative ways we can heal with tarot. The adaptability and usefulness of tarot is limited only by our imaginations. I predict the use of tarot for healing will continue to evolve and be an important part of the holistic health movement in the twenty-first century.

The pendulum swings

The holistic health movement provides a context in which true healing arts can flourish. But, as with most radical change, the pendulum has swung a bit too far: we are in danger of throwing the baby out with the bath water. I have met so many people who are *either* "alternative treatment advocates" *or* a "traditional medicine supporters." I am most discouraged by the black-and-white thinking of "us versus them" in choosing treatment.

I do not believe health care has to be an "either-or-all-or-nothing" choice, but rather, a careful blending of ancient and modern techniques. I hope that eventually the pendulum will swing back and settle somewhere closer to the middle. When this happens, we will see a merging and blending of the best that *both* traditional and holistic health care have to offer.

This blending will require an enormous amount of work done by committed people. Much of the work will be on the self as a practitioner of the healing arts. Powerful healing does not emerge from laboratories and technological advances. Rather, it is the use of self, in a loving and compassionate way, which provides us with our most powerful instrument for healing.

Hope and healing for the new millennium

We are at a place in health care where science, medicine, and spirituality can be embraced with healing attitudes to create new possibilities for all of us. As the attitude of healing advances, the emphasis will be on achieving maximum wellness. Some hospitals already have "wellness centers": attached sites where people can go for nontraditional treatment and still be covered by insurance. My hope is that hospitals will be replaced by "healing centers," where the focus will be prevention of disease, self-responsibility, and viewing illness as an opportunity for growth.

In this setting, healing will evolve from the focus on the body to a focus on body, mind, and spirit. Therapy will include all that is now considered alternative treatment while retaining all that is good with technological medicine. The best of antiquity will be combined with the best of modern practices. What is good about Western medicine and its future? Plenty. Leukemia will never claim another child's life. The cure for cancer and AIDS will be found. Spinal cord injuries will be repaired and people will walk again.

But instead of being focused solely on repair of the broken body, technological medicine will be embued with the compassion of ancient practices: healing was to make whole. The concept of healing as making whole will create an atmosphere where curing and caring have equal importance. When this happens, we will have come full circle and truly be "back to the future."

I hope the pages of this book become dog-eared, highlighted, marked, and otherwise scribbled upon. *Tarot for the Healing Heart* is not useful to me unless it is useful to you. Let an intuitive creative force guide you as you listen to the message of dis-ease and discover the heart of healing.

Notes to Chapter 7

1. Giles, Cynthia. *The Tarot: Methods, Mastery and More* (New York: A Fireside Book, Simon and Schuster, 1996), pp. 209–210.

Chapter 8

Healing Heart Tarot: Life Lessons, Life Wisdom

*Question: Three birds are sitting in a tree, and two decide
to fly away. How many birds are left in the tree?
Answer: Three, because there's a difference between
deciding and doing.*

A gentle reminder

Tarot for the Healing Heart complements, but does not replace, standard medical care. Tarot work supplements professional care, bringing the unconscious mind into harmony with the physical self to assist the healing process. Treatment arrests the physical disease cycle and often buys precious time for real healing to occur on the emotional, psychological, and spiritual levels. If you are ill, contact the health professional of your choice before proceeding with any activity in this book.

The dance of life

Tarot cards are not "good" or "bad." They symbolize a spectrum of life experiences and every card presents an opportunity to learn and grow. The cyclical pattern of birth, growth, maturation, decay, death, and rebirth is the dance of illness and health—and the dance of life.

All cards in a healing layout are to be interpreted as right side up. If a reversed (upside down) card appears, it serves only to call attention to itself. It is saying, "Hey, look at me because I'm different. Examine me first because I'm the most important card in your layout." A reversed card may also mean the message is on an unconscious or psychological level, unknown to you. The message of the card may require meditation or dream work to make itself apparent.

Don't be concerned if your deck has Justice as No. 8 and Strength as No. 11 (traditionally, you will see Strength as No. 8). For the purposes of healing work, the meanings of both cards remain the same, regardless of the numbering.

Not all the meanings of a card will pertain to your situation. Choose one to three phrases that ring true and work with them first. As a rule, a tarot card will either tell you about a situation or give you advice about a situation. Consider your own insights, meanings, and images and how they might apply to your life. In healing work, the cards are used for insight and growth, not fortunetelling.

Life lesson

The *life lessons* of energy imbalance describe the messages of illness and dis-ease. With every card, ask yourself about its life lesson: What is the message of my dis-ease? Where is my pain? How does my pain or discomfort express itself? At what level is my life lesson most apparent (physical, emotional, psychological, or spiritual)? What am I to learn? What is out of balance in my life?

Note: To get familiar with the healing layouts, use life lesson descriptions when working with Part 2, "Lion Heart: understanding illness and listening to the message." The actions and inner wisdom questions can enhance any reading in the book. Healing is not tidy and sometimes the lines between lesson and wisdom blur. As you grow comfortable with the tarot work, use any phrase, suggestion, or question that rings true, regardless of the layout's placement.

Life wisdom

The *life wisdom* of energy in balance describes the healing process and healing action to take on your own behalf. With every card, ask yourself about its life wisdom: What choices can I make to release the healer within? How will this healing energy restore order to my life? What is the form my healing will take? What loving (healing) action can I take to start the healing process? What level of healing needs my attention now? What assistance do I need? What will support the healing process? What will make me whole and happy?

Note: At first, use *life wisdom* descriptions when working with Part 3, "Heart and Soul: understanding healing and support for the healing process." The actions and inner wisdom questions can clarify any reading in the book. Life lessons and wisdom often overlap. Feel free to use any phrase, suggestion, or question that feels right and beneficial to you when working with the tarot activities.

Getting the most from healing heart tarot

Each card's entry is followed by examples of action to take on your own behalf that will support the healing process. Questions at the end of each entry help you contact your inner wisdom through journaling or meditation. New insights will assist you in releasing the creative healer within. Use the suggestions and questions as launching points for your personal discovery as you learn to soar to a higher overview.

SECTION A: THE MAJOR ARCANA

The Major Arcana ("Greater Secrets"), Numbers 0–21, The Fool through The World, speaks to you of both life lessons and life wisdom: those qualities being tested and developed, your gifts and challenges, karma, and the reasons you are here. The twenty-two cards symbolize spiritual development and help you understand your place in the world.

The Greater Secrets will point to the higher overview of illness and healing and give you insights into the big picture. They will also hint at your ability to heal. If you listen carefully, you will be able to hear directions for healing.

The Fool (0)
MISTRUST (life lesson) / TRUST (life wisdom)

Life lesson (energy imbalance/dis-ease): Not listening to your inner voice; fearing or doubting the future; having a blind naiveté (immaturity or foolishness) which allows others to take advantage of you; refusing to try the new; lacking playfulness.

Life wisdom (balanced energy/healing): Having an openness to divine guidance based on trust; having spontaneity and a sense of playfulness; willing to take risks and try something new without knowing the outcome because you trust the process; abandoning old ways of thinking.

Actions to support the healing process: Try a sampling of several healing techniques (both ancient and modern) until you find the ones you trust. Everything you experience will lead you deeper into understanding who you are and what you believe. Take the time to play. Be spontaneous. Open your eyes, mind, and heart for a time of unfolding and divine guidance. Take a leap of faith.

Contacting your inner wisdom: Where am I being naive? Do I need to play more? What do I mistrust in my life? Where am I rigid?

The Magician (1)
LACK OF FOCUS (life lesson) / FOCUS (life wisdom)

Life lesson (imbalance/dis-ease): Lacking focus; indirectness; abusing power for selfish gain; at the worst, the Magician is dishonest about motives and can be destructive in relationships.

Life wisdom (balanced energy/healing): Being able to prioritize and make a choice; being able to focus your energy effectively to accomplish your goals; the ability to visualize your goals clearly; discovering the creator within.

Actions to support the healing process: As shaman, The Magician suggests alternative medical care and healers of all types. Seek esoteric and metaphysical knowledge. Be conscious of your ability to move energy through concentrated will (a.k.a. magic). Visualize a goal, make a plan, and get to work. Attend to the wisdom of your higher self through meditation. Do something creative.

Contacting your inner wisdom: Where do I need to focus my efforts? What are my goals in life? How can I be more creative?

The High Priestess (2)
SUPERFICIALITY (life lesson) / INTUITION (life wisdom)

Life lesson (imbalance/dis-ease): Being too literal or intellectual; an inability to trust intuition; an inability to acknowledge the masculine/feminine aspect of the personality; being vague or so caught up in your intuitive nature that you have difficulty living in the real, day-to-day world; disliking women.

Life wisdom (balanced energy/healing): Having complete faith in your intuition; making logical decisions based on your intuition; involvement with a group of women; seeking hidden knowledge through dreams, images, feelings, art, tarot, or astrology; seeking a counselor to help you explore things unseen.

Actions to support the healing process: Join a women's spirituality or support group. Heed your dreams. Study tarot or astrology. Take an art class. Get professional counseling. Request a healing dream. Accept no diagnosis at face value—get a second opinion. If a treatment doesn't feel right to you, get more information before proceeding because facts may be hidden. Pay attention to intuition in your daily life. Attend to your spiritual growth.

Contacting your inner wisdom: Am I relying too little or too much on my intuition? What masculine and feminine qualities need to be acknowledged? What are my relationships like with women? What memories or conflicts from childhood could apply to my situation today?

The Empress (3)

SMOTHERING (life lesson) / MOTHERING (life wisdom)

Life lesson (imbalance/dis-ease): Being a controlling, powerful woman; focused on others so much that self-nurturance is neglected; being unable to let go of relationships; emotional neediness; dwelling on the pains of the past; holding on to destructive situations and relationships.

Life wisdom (balanced energy/healing): The archetype of the Great Mother; now is the time to establish yourself in relationship to others; she is the part of you who knows how to create what you need; a time to nourish yourself as well as others; the creator within; a time to get in touch with your body and sensuality.

Actions to support the healing process: Set aside time every day to nurture your body, be it exercise or bubble baths. Evaluate your nutritional status and make changes when needed. Become aware of which foods drain your energy and avoid them. Do something that nurtures your creative soul on a regular basis.

   If you could be pregnant, get a test to confirm it and start prenatal care immediately. Spend more time with your children, family, and creative projects. You could benefit from gardening and connecting with Mother Earth, animals, and plants. Go to an art museum. Give yourself credit for your successes.

Contacting your inner wisdom: Look closely at the destructive and draining relationships that you maintain. Do I nurture myself on a regular basis? Do I feel conflict about the image of "Mother"?

The Emperor (4)

RIGIDITY (life lesson) / STABILITY (life wisdom)

Life lesson (imbalance/dis-ease): Being disenchanted with life; out of touch with feelings; rigidity; aggression; controlling father-figure; stubbornness.

Life wisdom (balance of energy/healing): Building something real and solid; assertiveness; having a clear-eyed view of reality; giving form and structure to your life; accepting responsibility for your actions; using logic to problem solve; loving father-figure; leadership abilities, especially at work.

Actions to support the healing process: Follow traditional treatments and therapies. You believe in your physician's ability to heal you. If you take supplements, you will probably do so secretively because you don't want your physician's disapproval. Everything is by the book and, for the most part, you follow all rules. Use logical reasoning when evaluating your current situation. Exercise your leadership abilities. Take charge of your life.

Contacting your inner wisdom: Describe your experiences with your own father. Is it time to separate off and make your own way in the world? Check your behavior for signs of stubbornness or lack of responsibility.

The Hierophant (5)

FANATICISM (life lesson) / INNER CONSCIENCE (life wisdom)

Life lesson (imbalance/dis-ease): Intolerance toward people whose religious viewpoint differs from yours; adopting principles without thinking them through; going against your true beliefs in order to gain acceptance of a group; blind faith; lacking an inner guide.

Life wisdom (balanced energy/healing): Having an inner conscience; searching for a spiritual or personal philosophy that is accessible through word, book, lecture, or service; having a carefully thought out and studied personal philosophy that guides you rather than rules you.

Actions to support the healing process: Seek the aid of regular treatment—this can be conventional or nontraditional, but the important thing is the ritualized attention to it. Believe in your body's ability to heal itseif and in your own power to attract the healer you need. Attend to your spiritual self and participate in ritual and ceremony. Look for spiritual ideas through the written word.

Don't be surprised if you find yourself following the tenets of a "guru"—you are looking for the visible face of divinity, be it God or Goddess, here on earth. Review the principles of established religion for insights into your current situation. Ask your inner teacher for guidance.

Contacting your inner wisdom: Do I examine the beliefs of a group before I join the group? Do I make regular contact with my healer within?

The Lovers (6)
DISHARMONY (life lesson) / RESPONSIBLE CHOICES (life wisdom)

Life lessons (imbalance/dis-ease): Being unable to make a choice; feeling cut off from guidance; not loving yourself; choosing irresponsibly; refusing to look at life's opposites; unable to trust love or risk losing control.

Life wisdom (balanced energy/healing): Understanding that both the intellect and intuition are important for guidance; making responsible choices, especially in relationships; becoming aware of the loving nature of your Higher Self; making a responsible decision about a love relationship; looking to your Higher Self for guidance; the ability to negotiate.

Actions to support the healing process: Seek to identify the opposites that need to be balanced in your situation. Look at all aspects of a situation to understand the implications of the choices you are making. Try out various therapies, both conventional and complementary. It's time to make choices about going through with medical procedures or changes in lifestyle.

Take seminars and workshops on the practical application of metaphysics. Get a past-life reading to help you heal a current issue. Look to your higher consciousness for guidance.

Contacting your inner wisdom: Where do I need to negotiate? Do I take responsibility for my choices? What is the loving thing to do?

The Chariot (7)
INNER CONFLICT (life lesson) / INNER CONTROL (life wisdom)

Life lessons (imbalance/dis-ease): Not understanding or controlling the opposites within you; inflated ego; lack of self-control; not having a sense of direction in your life; wanting to control others; aggression.

Life wisdom (balanced energy/healing): Solving a present problem using the skills of your past experiences; resolution of quarrels and conflict; self-control that is based on introspection; seeking to express the soul outwardly through work.

Actions to support the healing process: You are starting to open psychically—find the appropriate tools and books to enhance your capabilities. Attend workshops and seminars that support self-discovery. Visit powerful places in nature. Take it easy and slow down—preventive medicine is your goal. Accept your aggressive drives and learn to channel them into appropriate action. Harness your excess energy into constructive outlets.

Contacting your inner wisdom: Are there past issues that I need to consider and resolve before charging ahead? What inner struggle needs resolution?

Strength (8)
RAGE (life lesson) / COMPASSION (life wisdom)

Life lessons (imbalance/dis-ease): Lack of courage or integrity; destructive aggression; rage, possibly expressed in abusiveness or sexual abuse; lack of compassion; denying or being afraid of your instinctual (or animal) nature.

Life wisdom (balanced energy/healing): Making peace with the dark side of your nature and extending that compassion to others; having courage, strength, and self-discipline; psychic centers are about to open; having an inner strength that allows you to heal yourself and others.

Actions to support the healing process: Correct unhealthful dietary and lifestyle habits, for now is the time to heal yourself. You have the strength to do so. Keep a journal because you will benefit from seeing your thoughts on paper. Honor your masculine will power and your feminine intuition. Listen to other people's ideas and learn how to blend them with yours.

Contacting your inner wisdom: Where do I need to be more compassionate? In what ways can I make my animal nature a peaceful companion?

The Hermit (9)

FEAR OF THE DARK (life lesson) / SELF-AWARENESS (life wisdom)

Life lessons (imbalance/dis-ease): Fear of isolation and boredom; fear of introspection; spiritual emptiness; overdependence on a psychic counselor, tarot reader, or astrologer; unable to accept aging or death; impatience; depression; indecision.

Life wisdom (balanced energy/healing): Seeking solitude to find inner strength; accepting the natural rhythm of life, including aging and death; finding an individual light when established religions fail you; a spiritual climb that makes you a lantern in the dark for others; seeking the advice of a psychic, tarot reader, or astrologer; having inner wisdom; using meditation as a way to understanding; finding a mentor and learning from his or her experience.

Actions to support the healing process: Seek the advice of a psychic, tarot reader, or astrologer. Search for symbolism in your physical ailments—they are metaphors for work you need to do in a particular area of your life. Go on a spiritual retreat or spend a weekend alone with the TV and radio off: meditate, journal, seek your own wise counsel. Take a self-enrichment class.

Contacting your inner wisdom: Do I seek retreat from everyday routines and reevaluate my priorities? At what crossroads do I find myself?

Wheel of Fortune (10)
BLAME (life lesson) / ACCEPTING CHANGE (life wisdom)

Life lessons (imbalance/dis-ease): Believing yourself to be a victim of fate; feeling stuck in a rut; fighting change; not recognizing opportunities; unable to finish what you start; missing the big picture; holding on to the past.

Life wisdom (balanced energy/healing): Understanding that there is an orderly plan behind the seemingly random changes of your life; accepting the cyclical nature of time and change; a fortunate new beginning; seeing opportunity; determining how past events affect your present situation.

Actions to support the healing process: Become attuned to your own natural cycles and live by them. Clean up any emotional situations that you may have left hanging. Open up and speak your mind to avoid emotional and psychological imbalances. You will benefit from a regular exercise routine to literally increase your flexibility.

Contacting your inner wisdom: Am I prepared to go with the flow? Am I alert to unexpected opportunities when they knock?

Justice (11)

IMBALANCE (life lesson) / BALANCE (life wisdom)

Life lessons (imbalance/dis-ease): Leaping to a hasty decision without weighing all the factors; lack of balance in your life; using only cold logic to make a decision; not being able to weigh and balance difficult decisions; prejudice; being illogical.

Life wisdom (balanced energy/healing): Having the ability to make adjustments in your life; weighing and balancing difficult decisions; setting things right; seeking legal advice; if you've been ignoring what needs to be done, Justice will bring it into consciousness and you'll have an opportunity to take appropriate action.

Actions to support the healing process: Moderate your activities and avoid excesses of any kind. The name of the healing game with Justice is balance in all things. You may need to seek the advice of a lawyer to set things right. Avoid extremes in anything. Consider several viewpoints before making a decision about your health care. Weigh and balance difficult situations before taking action.

Contacting your inner wisdom: Where is my life out of balance and how can I restore harmony? What do I need to set right?

The Hanged Man (12)
PRIDE (life lesson) / HUMILITY (life wisdom)

Life lessons (imbalance/dis-ease): Being "hung up" by circumstances where old behaviors are no longer working; rigidly holding on to old values; an unwillingness to make the necessary sacrifices or do the work necessary for success; sacrificing too much of yourself.

Life wisdom (balanced energy/healing): Being able to look at something from another angle; being willing to make a sacrifice for a larger goal; deliberate turning toward the Higher Self and asking for help; allowing things to happen without the need to control; understanding that a reversal of fortune can challenge you to grow stronger.

Actions to support the healing process: Look at your situation from another viewpoint before making decisions about treatment. If you have a long-term health problem, try a new approach and change doctors if you need to. You may have a complete change of viewpoint about your health—if you've been using only complementary therapies, switch to conventional ones and vice versa.

Research and be willing to experiment until you feel satisfied. Realize that a sacrifice may have to be made in your healing—you may have to give up something you enjoy to get well.

Contacting your inner wisdom: Where do I get hung up? What do I need to look at differently?

Death (13)

STAGNATION (life lesson) / TRANSFORMATION (life wisdom)

Life lessons (imbalance/dis-ease): Blocking out sad feelings; fearing change and allowing that fear to control you; physical or mental stagnation.

Life wisdom (balanced energy/healing): Letting go of the old to make way for the new; being comforted during a sad time with valid insights; being open to change and the opportunities it brings.

Actions to support the healing process: Let go of old habits or thought patterns that were once useful but are now outdated. If you have any unresolved grief, see a counselor who can help you with your mourning.

Physical symptoms associated with this card have to do with a resistance to letting go and retention of old ways. You may have problems with constipation (resistance to letting go) or fluid retention. Recognize these irritating problems are a call from your higher self to pay attention to the message of dis-ease.

Contacting your inner wisdom: What cycle do I need to finish? In what ways am I changing?

Temperance (14)
OVERINDULGENCE (life lesson) / EASY DOES IT (life wisdom)

Life lessons (imbalance/dis-ease): Not allowing emotions to flow, so they get stuck in depression or erupt in violence; denying a dialogue between yourself and your higher consciousness; taking action without thought to the consequences; overindulgence and addictions.

Life wisdom (balanced energy/healing): Striving for emotional balance; knowing your resources; deciding to do something because you want to test yourself; taking a moderate approach—easy does it, but do it; allowing the healing process to unfold in its own time; the healer within.

Actions to support the healing process: Write "Easy does it—but do it" on a piece of paper and place it where you will see it every day. Moderation and self-restraint in all things improves your health—don't overdo. Consult a healer—don't be surprised if you encounter a healer at exactly the time you need one. Become a volunteer for a cause you believe in. Meditation will greatly improve your outlook.

Contacting your inner wisdom: Where are my emotions out of balance? Am I paying attention to psychic insights? Do I know my resources? In what way am I freely testing myself?

The Devil (15)

FEAR-SEPARATION (life lesson) / CONNECTEDNESS (life wisdom)

Life lessons (imbalance/dis-ease): Being chained to your fears; failure to love yourself; being chained to material goods; having an issue with power—controlling or being controlled; separating off from your spiritual self; the inability to play; cutting yourself off from others; being the aggressor; repressed sexuality.

Life wisdom (balanced energy/healing): Removing the blocks of fear and separateness; understanding your own light side/dark side which leads to compassion for others; finding a spiritual life; accepting your need to lighten up and play; learning to love yourself and others; expressing your sexuality with joy; feeling connected to other people and less to material goods.

Actions to support the healing process: Lighten up and play. Do healthful things that you enjoy. Get enough sleep. Seek the guidance of a counselor to help you through negative thought patterns, depression, and fear. Evaluate your need for material goods and your attitudes toward work and money.

Exercise will help you get out of your head—by being in touch with your body, you will improve your sex drive. Evaluate your use of alcohol and/or drugs—get help to stop if their use is interfering with your work, money, relationships, responsibilities—and life.

Contacting your inner wisdom: What is my attitude toward work and money? Is the use of alcohol and/or drugs interfering with my ability to function? What is my attitude toward sex? What do I fear?

The Tower (16)
DESTRUCTION (life lesson) / LIBERATION (life wisdom)

Life lessons (imbalance/dis-ease): Having false philosophies or old goals which prevent you from seizing new opportunities; avoidance of change; falling apart or breaking down when things change; releasing repressed energy in an angry or destructive way.

Life wisdom (balanced energy/healing): Breaking down unhealthy beliefs to liberate your true self; having a flash of illumination; breaking through old ways of thinking; releasing repressed energy that is exciting and dynamic; finding inner strength and spiritual meaning in tragedy and loss.

Actions to support the healing process: Meditation will help you find meaning in tragedy and loss. Join a support group to strengthen the healing process. Soul searching will provide you with answers to the unanswerable.

It is time to be careful; use caution, as you may have a tendency toward accidents (sudden change) or car problems. Symptoms of illness will appear suddenly. Prevention (taking good care of yourself) is the best medicine.

Contacting your inner wisdom: Am I holding on to beliefs that complicate my situation? Have I had a sudden flash of insight?

The Star (17)
DESPAIR (life lesson) / HOPE (life wisdom)

Life lessons (imbalance/dis-ease): Failing to recognize your talents and abilities; loss of hope; loss of self-esteem; getting lost in wishful thinking, lacking faith; lack of self-confidence.

Life wisdom (balanced energy/healing): An opportunity for new insight into a situation; gaining a sense of direction; having a renewed sense of hope; inspiration; discovering the inner light; the healing heart.

Actions to support the healing process: Continue to seek and actively participate in treatment for chronic illness—do anything that helps you maintain a sense of hope. Alternative therapies will be beneficial. Retreats and spas will renew your spirit. Attend seminars and read books that inspire you and encourage hope.

Give of yourself in service to others and there you will find meaning. You may have out-of-body experiences at this time because The Star is symbolically linked to Aquarius—read all you can about astral travel. Align yourself with your higher consciousness through meditation.

Contacting your inner wisdom: What do I hope for? What do I do for myself that renews my spirit?

The Moon (18)
CONFUSION (life lesson) / MYSTERY (life wisdom)

Life lessons (imbalance/dis-ease): A time of doubt and confusion about your feelings; a feeling of madness; an uncomfortable fluctuation between feelings; indecision; mood swings, depression; not trusting intuition or feelings

Life wisdom (balanced energy/healing): Realizing solutions may be intuitive rather than logical; being open to information from dreams; trusting feelings and intuition; being open to the mysteries of your life; feeling guided or pulled to some predetermined purpose; recognizing the changes and cycles of your life.

Actions to support the healing process: Work on developing and trusting your intuition. You may have premonitions about illness—if you suspect a problem based on intuitive insight, seek professional help because you will be right. Have all lumps and cysts biopsied. Get a second opinion if a diagnosis doesn't feel right to you. Explore alternative treatments.

Past-life work helps you remember events that give meaning to your current health problems. Menstruation may be heavy—pay attention to your cycles and get treatment if you need it. Request a healing dream—it will have the power to heal through insight.

Contacting your inner wisdom: Do I trust and follow my intuition? What am I being pulled toward? Am I open to information from my dreams and memories?

The Sun (19)

BURNOUT (life lesson) / GOLDEN UNDERSTANDING (life wisdom)

Life lessons (imbalance/dis-ease): Burnout; burning your candle at both ends; feeling no joy in life; keeping secrets that eventually burn you; overcoming people with your energy and personality.

Life wisdom (balanced energy/healing): Success; optimism, positive energy and action; to become a child again and see the world with joy; calm self-confidence; a time of clear vision.

Actions to support the healing process: Engage in playful activities that bring you joy. If you are burning the candle at both ends, start delegating responsibility, saying no, prioritizing, and letting go. Seek professional help for feelings of burnout.

Spending time in the sun will energize you. (Use sunscreen, of course.) Do not ignore burning feelings in your chest—you need treatment. Eat nutritional foods for extra energy. If you feel "fired up" to try something new, follow your desire.

Contacting your inner wisdom: How can I shine my light on others? Do I energize or overwhelm others?

Judgement (20)
PAYING THE PIPER (life lesson) / REBIRTH (life wisdom)

Life lessons (imbalance/dis-ease): Having a harsh inner critic; seeking revenge or divine retribution on someone who has hurt you; being critical of others; seeking to punish, as in paying the piper.

Life wisdom (balanced energy/healing): Making amends; paying debts that need to be paid; an honest and sincere self-appraisal; reaping what you have sown; an integration of the light side/dark side that lifts you into spiritual understanding; compassion; healing.

Actions to support the healing process: If you have been holding a grudge or refusing to apologize, make amends now. Seek counseling if you are having difficulty forgiving yourself for your past mistakes: this lack of forgiveness is making you ill. Transforming your ideas will help you see what is possible, especially with long-term dis-ease or disability. Get a past-life reading—you may be dealing with karmic issues.

Contacting your inner wisdom: Do I judge myself and others harshly? Do I need to make amends? Whom or what do I need to forgive?

The World (21)

CHASING A RAINBOW / SOARING TO THE HIGHER OVERVIEW

Life lessons (imbalance/dis-ease): Looking for happiness outside yourself; wishful thinking; chasing impossible rainbows; repressing painful memories; hanging on to the past; unable to see the big picture.

Life wisdom (balanced energy/healing): The completion of one cycle and the beginning of another; standing on solid ground inside yourself; integration of the shadow; realizing your goals; seeing life as a process; soaring to the higher overview of illness and healing.

Actions to support the healing process: Seek a holistic practitioner—someone who understands that the whole is greater than the sum of its parts. Make time for yourself each day—you need to stop and smell the roses. Step back from your current situation in order to see the big picture.

If you are frozen by indecision because all choices look acceptable, simply choose one and act upon it. It doesn't matter which one you select—the important thing is that you take action on your own behalf. Pay special attention to coincidences—they are your higher self's way of guiding you to beneficial health practices.

Contacting your inner wisdom: Do I trust my inner wisdom? What will help me soar to the higher overview of my life? What new cycle am I beginning?

SECTION B: THE MINOR ARCANA

The Minor Arcana, or "Lesser Secrets," offer information along the four levels of illness and health: Pentacles: physical reality and the body; Cups: emotions and feelings; Swords: psychological well-being; and Wands: spiritual creativity in everyday life.

In illness and healing, there is no separation between body, emotion, mind, and spirit. It is impossible to be ill without all four levels of existence being affected. It is likewise impossible to heal without attending to these same four levels of being.

Illness does not fall neatly into categories. Because illness at any level affects all levels, the lines sometimes blur. The following descriptions are intended to serve as only general guides as you begin to look for answers.

Pentacles: the body of illness and health

Suit of Tarot	Pentacles
Element	Earth
Level of illness or healing	Physical body, instincts, work, money, security

Ace of Pentacles (1)
Beginnings, an upsurge of energy on the physical plane

Life lessons (imbalance/dis-ease): Being off-center; having a false sense of security; competitive where money is concerned; feeling stuck; overdependence on security and comfort.

Life wisdom (balanced energy/healing): Being centered; a time to manifest in the material world; financial assistance; a business or work opportunity; the beginning of a new enterprise.

Actions to support the healing process: If you have been floundering, it's time to refocus your goals. Read *Creating a Life Worth Living: A Practical Course in Career Design* by Carol Lloyd (HarperCollins, 1997).

    Consult an herbalist and eat your vegetables. Commune with nature. Consider outdoor exercise. Try a spa that offers mineral and mud baths. Meditation will ground you. Get involved with an environmental cause you believe in.

Contacting your inner wisdom: What are my attitudes toward work and money? How do I feel about my body? What do I value?

Two of Pentacles (2)
Balance or the need for balance on the physical plane

Life lessons (imbalance/dis-ease): Walking a tightrope; feeling out-of-balance; juggling time; clinging to one position; fake lightheartedness; failing to consider another viewpoint.

Life wisdom (balanced energy/healing): Adaptability; flexibility; balance; skillful manipulation of many factors to achieve success.

Actions to support the healing process: Now is the time to make changes in your life, but don't try to control the outcomes. Roll with the punches—if you maintain flexibility, all will be well. Most of your physical complaints are stress related from doing the juggling act. See what aspect of your life you have been neglecting and reevaluate your priorities for more balance.

Have some fun—you've been serious for too long. Yoga will help you with any muscle stiffness. You may start to discover the holistic view of health—mind and body really are connected. Try to draw spiritual meaning from the daily tasks of life.

Contacting your inner wisdom: How do I adapt to change? Am I able to balance work with play?

Three of Pentacles (3)
Growth and expansion on the physical plane

Life lessons (imbalance/dis-ease): Laziness; not following through on a work situation; a situation (including a health condition) gradually getting worse through neglect.

Life wisdom (balanced energy/healing): Initial completion of a project with much hard effort to follow; beginning to recognize the spiritual aspects of work; producing something worthwhile. A situation (including health) gradually improving with time.

Actions to support the healing process: Recognize that your body is where your spirit lives—start taking care of it. You will benefit from "building" an altar, a sanctuary for your inner self. Make it a physical expression of your spirituality. For healing, it needs to appeal to your senses—vibrant colors, rich scents, plush textures.

You have skills and abilities—use them to find a path of spiritual growth through work. Not liking your work will make you sick. If you do not enjoy your job, it is time to find one that gives you more personal satisfaction.

Contacting your inner wisdom: Do I see the spiritual value of my work? What am I working toward?

Four of Pentacles (4)
Stability or stagnation on the physical level

Life lessons (imbalance/dis-ease): Miserliness in money or spirit; using money to insulate from the outside world; greed; blocking out feelings; lack of emotional generosity—Mr. Scrooge.

Life wisdom (balanced energy/healing): The ability to establish personal boundaries; protection of self; giving life structure; saving money and resources; making every effort count.

Actions to support the healing process: Get an outside opinion of your situation because your viewpoint is narrow at this time. If you are giving too much of yourself away (especially paired with the Queen of Wands), set limits and learn to say no. If you have been isolated, a group activity or hobby (especially related to getting you outdoors) will put you with other people and give you more confidence and security.

Your health may be bound up with attitudes and beliefs about money and you may experience migraines and constipation because of it. Counseling will help you learn when and how to let go and your symptoms will improve.

Contacting your inner wisdom: What emotions, attitudes, or beliefs should I release? Do I need to ask for help?

Five of Pentacles (5)
Conflict, struggle on the physical level

Life lessons (imbalance/dis-ease): Feelings of abandonment; living with basic survival issues of food, clothing, shelter, and poor health; homelessness; loss of any kind; struggling against problems alone when outside forces are of no help; hitting bottom.

Life wisdom (balanced energy/healing): Paying attention to detail; something of value is found in a painful situation; through hardship inner meaning is found; realizing help is available and asking for it; climbing back up after hitting bottom.

Actions to support the healing process: The stress level in your life is high due to financial worries or deep loss and you have physical ailments and fatigue to prove it. You may feel your spirit is broken and life has lost its meaning. You seek the guidance of a spiritual adviser, but she or he is disappointing.

Focus on yourself—purify, cleanse, and rebalance your body. Ritual will help give you structure. Dig in and hold on—things will gradually improve. There is probably a financial source that you have been overlooking—do some research.

Help for basic survival issues is available if you actively search for it. Swallow your pride—ask for help and you'll receive it.

Contacting your inner wisdom: What am I doing to help myself? What untapped resource is eluding me?

Six of Pentacles (6)
Harmony on the physical plane

Life lessons (imbalance/dis-ease): Feelings of depletion; poor money management; holding someone a financial hostage: expecting favors for lending money; insensitivity to the needs of others.

Life wisdom (balanced energy/healing): Drawing to you what you need; a healing by giving; sharing and generosity that restores faith; that which we give away returns to us threefold.

Actions to support the healing process: Exchange energy—share your resources and wisdom with those in need. By sharing, you will attract what you need. Keep your insurance policy current. The Six of Pentacles often means your medical bills are paid through insurance or the generosity of others.

Ask for help. Touch therapy and massage will benefit you. Study the healing arts—your gift is the ability to heal by giving to others.

Contacting your inner wisdom: What is my attitude toward giving and receiving help? How do I nurture myself?

Seven of Pentacles (7)
Inner work on the physical plane

Life lessons (imbalance/dis-ease): Indecision; feeling discouraged; failing to evaluate progress at regular intervals; being in conflict about ambition and other values.

Life wisdom (balanced energy/healing): Deciding between material security and fulfillment of desire; trusting the process of growth; assessing mistakes to learn from them; being a practical dreamer.

Actions to support the healing process: Time-outs are good, but you need to reorganize your priorities and decide upon a course of action. Sustained effort is needed to fulfill your dreams. Take stock of your health habits—make a plan to change the ones that are no longer useful to you.

Because you have been in a state of indecision for awhile, attend a seminar or read a book about manifesting your goals. Meditate with the Magician to help you visualize and create the future you've been dreaming about.

Contacting your inner wisdom: What do I want to be when I grow up? What are my expectations of success?

Eight of Pentacles (8)

Regeneration and new ways forward on the physical plane

Life lessons (imbalance/dis-ease): Blowing out of a job because the work is not fulfilling; being a workaholic with subsequent burnout; ambition without the desire to work hard.

Life wisdom (balanced energy/healing): Starting over in a new profession; undertaking new work that is meaningful; concentrated effort; changing directions in midlife to find fulfillment.

Actions to support the healing process: Your current work is making you sick because it is not fulfilling. Released from the indecision of the Seven, you take action and retrain, go back to school, or change professions completely. Even though you may look childish or unstable to those who know you, you change directions and find your life's work.

A tough apprenticeship may be required and the extra effort keeps you off balance for awhile: if your energy sags during this busy time, rest, eat sensibly, and concentrate on the present moment. All the effort will be worth it—your nagging physical complaints disappear as you find balance in your life's work. Consider a hobby to add to your satisfaction in life.

Contacting your inner wisdom: What do I need to do to feel more satisfied with my life and work?

Nine of Pentacles (9)

Completion on the physical plane

Life lessons (imbalance/dis-ease): Financially secure, but being without purpose in life; depression; low self-esteem; boredom; imbalance between what we want and what we are willing to work for.

Life wisdom (balanced energy/healing): Self-esteem; financial stability that allows for the freedom of meaningful work; a woman who works alone by choice for the good of all; the ability to rely on oneself; finding spirituality in nature and animals.

Actions to support the healing process: The Nine of Pentacles is unique—no other card in the deck offers such strong energies of self-esteem and independence. Your task is to find a spiritual meaning for your affluence—how can you use your good fortune to help others and remain behind the scenes?

Seek answers to minor physical problems in self-help books. Spending time alone outdoors, gardening or with animals, will renew your spirit. Your path to spiritual fulfillment will be a solitary one and you use time alone to sort priorities. Your dreams and insightful meditations will have the power to heal.

Contacting your inner wisdom: Am I still seeking a purpose in life? What do I value?

Ten of Pentacles (10)

Starting over at a higher cycle on the physical plane

Life lessons (imbalance/dis-ease): One problem after another; being upset by someone close; lethargy; feelings of separation; the urge to risk everything due to impatience with the status quo; addictive gambling.

Life wisdom (balanced energy/healing): Being personally successful while contributing to society as a whole; what you value has lasting value to others; financial stability that builds a solid future; being rich in family tradition.

Actions to support the healing process: The key to future stability is to take an interest in family or community today. "Give back" to the next generation by becoming a Big Brother/Big Sister—what you value will have lasting value to others.

To attain spiritual meaning from financial security, look to understand the higher overview of what you do with your money, keeping future benefits in mind. Concentrate on the richness of daily life and look for hidden meaning in ordinary things.

Dream work will help you develop precognitive dreams because you are attuned to your higher self. You will benefit from studying clairvoyance, literally "clear sight" for the future.

Contacting your inner wisdom: How can I participate more in my family or community life? Am I willing to share my wisdom with others?

Cups: the emotions of illness and health

Suit of Tarot	Cups
Element	Water
Level of illness or healing	Emotions, feelings, intuition, dreams, imagination

Ace of Cups (1)

Beginnings, an upsurge of energy on the emotional plane

Life lessons (imbalance/dis-ease): Unhappiness caused by a failure to realize the emotional gifts of everyday life; reacting violently; not recognizing the higher overview

Life wisdom (balanced energy/healing): The opening of the heart; the opening of psychic, spiritual channels; self-nurturing; new relationships; new feelings.

Actions to support the healing process: Look for ways to express yourself with more feeling. Keep a journal of emotions, connecting the actual event/symptom with your feelings. See a counselor if you need help with troubling emotions.

Your physical health will improve in direct proportion to your emotional outlook. Meditation will open your heart to higher consciousness. The Ace of Cups is the gift of love—remain open to unexpected opportunities for emotional growth.

Contacting your inner wisdom: How can I express my abilities with more feeling? Am I open to new relationships (work, friendship, or romance)?

Two of Cups (2)

Balance or the need for balance on the emotional plane

Life lessons (imbalance/dis-ease): Possessiveness in a relationship; denial of our masculine/feminine personality; inability to commit to a relationship or partnership; uncooperative in partnerships.

Life wisdom (balanced energy/healing): Commitment and cooperation in relationships and partnerships; balanced emotions; acceptance of masculine/feminine qualities in our personality.

Actions to support the healing process: Listen with your heart when other people are expressing a different viewpoint—strive for understanding in all situations. Although you may not agree, "walking a mile in another's moccasins" will enrich you.

Think balance in all things: blood pressure, heart rate, sugar levels, work/play cycles, emotions—all need to be on an even keel for you to feel your best. Avoid extremes. Meditate to keep your heart chakra open.

Contacting your inner wisdom: How do I benefit from cooperation with others? Do I practice light-side/dark-side thinking?

Three of Cups (3)
Growth and expansion on the emotional plane

Life lessons (imbalance/dis-ease): Alcohol and/or drug dependence to alter feelings; overindulgence of any kind.

Life wisdom (balanced energy/healing): Time to celebrate; initial emotional work done with much work to follow, but for now, rejoice.

Actions to support the healing process: You've worked hard on yourself to be where you are—give credit where credit is due. Take a break or much-needed rest, relax, and play to renew your spirit and restore your health. If you've been overindulging in food, drink, or drugs, it's time to cut back. Seek outside support if you need it.

Contacting your inner wisdom: Do I use food, alcohol, or drugs to change the way I feel? Do I take the time to enjoy my accomplishments, relationships, and partnerships?

Four of Cups (4)

Stability or stagnation on the emotional plane

Life lessons (imbalance/dis-ease): Depression; boredom; resentment; withdrawal from emotions; confusion and hurt; loss of idealism.

Life wisdom (balanced energy/healing): Reevaluation of relationships that yields clarity; reality sets in after a period of idealism giving way to more realistic expectations.

Actions to support the healing process: Depression may be profound—seek professional assistance. "Re-feeling" will yield physical dis-eases. Have a cardiac checkup if you are experiencing chest pain or irregular heart beat—you may literally have a broken heart. As you unravel your confusion and change your emotional outlook, your physical symptoms will improve—a spiritual healer, psychologist, psychiatrist, or psychic will benefit you.

Contacting your inner wisdom: What am I feeling? How can I be more realistic in my expectations of myself and others?

Five of Cups (5)
Conflict, struggle on the emotional plane

Life lessons (imbalance/dis-ease): Disappointment on the verge of despair; focusing on loss rather than what is left; staying stuck in regret; wallowing in sorrow.

Life wisdom (balanced energy/healing): Choosing to focus on what is left after loss; seeing that all is not lost; looking within for emotional stability when situations appear to be hopeless.

Actions to support the healing process: Focusing on what might have been will cause dis-ease and leave you victimized, with a sense of powerlessness. For healing to begin, choose to focus on what you have, rather than what you've lost. By doing so you regain your power to heal.

    The cause of your dis-ease is primarily emotional. Emotional struggle indicates a counselor or therapist can help you sort through difficult feelings, especially a grief counselor. Letting go of past sorrow is your goal in treatment. Read all you can about grieving and grief work. If it's fitting to your spiritual beliefs, study the Crone aspect of the Goddess—She can teach you how to let go.

Contacting your inner wisdom: Is there a situation that needs to be released in love? What new avenues of self-expression will bring me joy?

Six of Cups (6)

Harmony on the emotional plane

Life lessons (imbalance/dis-ease): Clinging to old ideas; unwilling to change; unable to remember the past accurately because of emotional pain.

Life wisdom (balanced energy/healing): Seeing value in the past; making peace with the past in a realistic way.

Actions to support the healing process: People with post-traumatic stress disorder (PTSD) often get this card. Revisit the memories of childhood or a traumatic incident to see how events shaped your personality and emotional outlook. If you had serious trauma or abuse, a therapist is strongly indicated. You should never do this painful, but necessary, work alone.

A past-life reading or hypnosis can also reveal how memories are shaping you today. Welcome new ideas and self-expressive activities to help you heal old emotional wounds. Be kind to the wounded child who lives inside you.

Physical symptoms surfacing now may have roots in your past. Make sure your doctor has all your old records. Concentrate on any memories that give you a sense of safety. Study mythology and old religions. Your healing will be in rediscovering your past and finding value in it.

Contacting your inner wisdom: What do I need to do to heal a painful past? What memories give me comfort and safety? What new activities will help me move forward?

Seven of Cups (7)
Inner work on the emotional plane

Life lessons (imbalance/dis-ease): The "fairy dust" card—being stuck in fantasy and wishful thinking; indecision; Peter Pan.

Life wisdom (balanced energy/healing): Identifying false assumptions; recognizing golden opportunities and taking the time to consider what to do next; recognizing the complexity of emotions.

Actions to support the healing process: If you are feeling a bit spacey, practice grounding and centering. Boji stones and hematite will help ground your energy. You are in a period of indecision. You will benefit from sampling different types of alternative healing techniques because each one will have something to offer you.

    The mysticism of the seven implies you benefit from diversity—explore diverse new age philosophies. Analyze the illness in your life because you are ready to confront your deeper emotional nature. Keep a dream journal and practice visualization. Both will help you focus on skills and abilities. Formulate a plan to bring your dreams into reality.

Contacting your inner wisdom: How much work am I willing to put forth to make my dreams a reality? What opportunities have I lost because of daydreaming?

Eight of Cups (8)

Regeneration and new ways forward on the emotional plane

Life lessons (imbalance/dis-ease): Abandoning hope; a refusal to leave a situation; emotional withdrawal; filling others' needs to the point of exhaustion.

Life wisdom (balanced energy/healing): A painful, conscious act of letting go that takes you deeper into your spirituality; leaving the past behind; letting go of a situation or relationship after a long period of emotional investment.

Actions to support the healing process: Look for ways to incorporate spirituality into your daily life—meditation, study, visualization, voluntary solitude, any activity that strengthens your inner life. By centering and spending time alone, you forge a new link to your higher self.

Identify feelings of loss or regret and meditate on how you can do things differently from now on. You may find a grief ritual helpful to focus on the conscious act of letting go. Allow yourself to feel the sadness of grief, for it is in the grieving process that you will find the power to heal. Seek professional support if needed.

Contacting your inner wisdom: What do I want to leave behind? Do I need time off to rediscover my sense of self?

Nine of Cups (9)

Completion on the emotional plane

Life lessons (imbalance/dis-ease): Superficiality; being in a tangled or emotionally oppressive situation; lust; laziness; aimlessness.

Life wisdom (balanced energy/healing): Sometimes called the "wish fulfillment" card—letting yourself wish for whatever you want, knowing you deserve it; finding solace in ordinary pleasures; optimism.

Actions to support the healing process: The key to physical well-being is avoiding self-indulgence of any type. If weight is a problem, evaluate nutritional habits. Avoid excess sweets.

Meditation and creative visualization will help you formulate your goals and vision for the future. Consider using your talents in new ways. Focus on simple pleasures of everyday life—a sunset, time with friends, a beautiful day, a walk in the park. In simplicity you will find your dreams.

Contacting your inner wisdom: What satisfies me? How might I use my talents in more meaningful ways?

Ten of Cups (10)
Starting over at a higher cycle on the emotional plane

Life lessons (imbalance/dis-ease): An emotionally charged situation produces feelings of anger; failing to appreciate gifts from the heart; too much idealism in personal relationships.

Life wisdom (balanced energy/healing): Lasting contentment and peace; a gentle love that extends to others; a sense of permanence and future purpose; can indicate marriage and family; being "at home" with yourself and others.

Actions to support the healing process: Find ways to express gratitude for the positive relationships you have in your life—send those flowers, make the call, and write the note. Extend your positive feelings outward to the larger community by volunteering for a cause in which you can emotionally invest yourself.

Some of your health problems could have a basis in genetics. The Ten of Cups encourages you to explore your heritage. There you may find clues to perplexing health problems. Focus your spirituality on appreciation of divine gifts. The heart of your spiritual power is gratitude for all you have been given.

Contacting your inner wisdom: Do I take the time to appreciate all that I have? What does my family heritage have to teach me?

Swords: the power of the mind in illness and health

Suit of Tarot	Swords
Element	Air
Level of illness or healing	Psychological makeup, decisions, depression, conflict, pain, surgery, loss

Ace of Swords (1)
Beginnings, an upsurge of energy on the psychological plane

Life lessons (imbalance/dis-ease): Confused ideas; illusion; emotions controlling decisions; failure to think things through.

Life wisdom (balanced energy/healing): Victory over struggle; strength despite adversity; the gift of inner vision; an upsurge of mental activity with the power and force to win; change for the good; a card of great spiritual strength.

Actions to support the healing process: It's time to bring physical energy into balance with mental energy. Your symptoms are probably related to stress and anxiety. Take a class or study relaxation techniques to find a balanced sense of reality. Physical exercise will release excess emotion.

    Self-help books will assist you in piercing illusion as you search for understanding. A comparative or world religion class can uncover spiritual truths through intellectual study. Meditate with the Hierophant because it symbolizes a search for spirituality through the written word.

Contacting your inner wisdom: Do I need to analyze my situation more objectively? Do I get carried away with emotion?

Two of Swords (2)

Balance or the need for balance on the psychological plane

Life lessons (imbalance/dis-ease): An impasse or stalemate; inability to make a decision; procrastination; not wanting to confront the reality of a situation; blocking emotion.

Life wisdom (balanced energy/healing): Seeing the reality of a situation; making a painful decision that allows for change; getting off the fence of indecision and taking action.

Actions to support the healing process: Seeing the way things really are for the first time can be a shattering experience. Get outside support if you need it to deal with painful decisions. Fear, uncertainty, or blocked emotions may cause you to feel all the physical effects of tension.

Get a massage to stay in touch with your body. Deep breathing exercises will align you with Air, the element of this suit, to get things moving again. Meditation will quiet your very active mind. Life will resume its forward motion once you make a difficult decision that you've been putting off.

Contacting your inner wisdom: What decision do I need to make now? How can I reconcile conflicting thoughts and emotions?

Three of Swords (3)

Growth and expansion on the psychological plane

Life lessons (imbalance/dis-ease): Quarrels and conflict, especially in relationships; a broken heart; blocking the healing process; holding onto old pain; unresolved grief.

Life wisdom (balanced energy/healing): Letting go of something sad or painful; focusing on solutions instead of problems; acknowledging hurt, pain, or grief so that it can be faced and worked through.

Actions to support the healing process: This is a card of vision and understanding, (no pain, no gain), and carries the promise of psychological growth if problems are faced directly. A psychologist or counselor is indicated to help you sort through psychological blocks that are keeping you stuck in old thinking patterns. Acknowledge your pain, examine it, and look for ways to do things differently.

Consider ways to define your problem from another perspective, then focus on solutions rather than problems. Releasing old ideas will help you generate new ones. This card symbolizes the broken heart. Become heart-smart—evaluate your lifestyle and family history for cardiac risk factors and take action to reduce risk.

Contacting your inner wisdom: What do I need to finish so that I can move on? Can I accept reality and focus on solutions?

Four of Swords (4)

Stability or stagnation on the psychological plane

Life lessons (imbalance/dis-ease): Denying emotions; hiding from the world to avoid pain or confrontation; not acknowledging the need to rest.

Life wisdom (balanced energy/healing): Introspection; taking the time needed to heal and renew self; rest and recuperation after stress, especially after surgery; calm after the storm.

Actions to support the healing process: You need to take the time out required to heal or evaluate your present situation. Consider counseling if you can't work out problems on your own.

Take some time off and do something that feeds your soul. Read, study, and educate yourself in an introspective technique that appeals to your intellect (I Ching, numerology, or astrology are examples). Meditation will quiet your mind so that your body can heal.

Contacting your inner wisdom: Do I take the time I need to heal? What do I need to do to restore my energy?

Five of Swords (5)

Conflict, struggle on the psychological plane

Life lessons (imbalance/dis-ease): Despair felt after loss; using others as a
scapegoat (reason) for our own defeat; not accepting a no-win situation.

Life wisdom (balanced energy/healing): The freedom found in accepting
one's own limitations; making an apology; turning away from a struggle;
letting go of pride so forward progress can be made.

Actions to support the healing process: Set priorities—in any conflict,
ask yourself how important it is for you to win. In order to lift any
restrictions you have placed on yourself, you will need to take some
action on your own behalf. Aggressive tendencies can be channeled
into sports, martial arts, or aerobic exercise. (Get a check-up before
engaging in any new exercise regimen.)

Guard against turning anger against yourself in the form of self-
destructive habits. Stop spinning your wheels: withdraw from a conflict
to avoid making yourself sick—no good can come from wasting your
energy on a no-win situation. You always have the power of choice.

Contacting your inner wisdom: Does there have to be a winner and a loser in
this situation? Is my own pride holding me back from making progress?

Six of Swords (6)

Harmony on the psychological plane

Life lessons (imbalance/dis-ease): Unhappy memories; symbolic of a stormy spiritual/psychological journey; feeling stranded or stuck in deep water.

Life wisdom (balanced energy/healing): A journey toward peace after an agonizing decision; feeling guided in your decision-making process; making forward progress, especially in the area of communication.

Actions to support the healing process: Work on a long-standing (chronic) problem, be it physical or psychological. Chart your own course of action by listening to your inner voice. A period of painful, but honest, communication can begin the healing process.

A troubling relationship (personal or professional) has gone along quietly for a long time because of your silence. If you decide to do something about it, get a neutral third party to mediate communications.

You may have to travel to get the health care support you need. Your healing will be gradual—slow, steady progress as you put distance between you and a painful past.

Contacting your inner wisdom: What do I need to leave behind so I can concentrate on growth? What do I need to communicate for healing to begin?

Seven of Swords (7)
Inner work on the psychological plane

Life lessons (imbalance/dis-ease): Using deception to get what you want; dishonesty in communications; avoiding face-to-face confrontation; an unwillingness to ask for help; an impulsive act when careful planning is required.

Life wisdom (balanced energy/healing): Using "brains, not brawn" in a confrontational situation; prudence; nothing is accomplished by aggression.

Actions to support the healing process: Which course of action will support the healing process—acting in isolation or asking for help? Only you can decide.

    If you need advice, you will find it in a reader, therapist, or friend. This card carries a warning of possible deception: be wary of any health practitioner who suggests many expensive interventions or treatments. Get a second opinion before spending your money.

Contacting your inner wisdom: Do I think for myself? Recall a situation where you had to act in way that went against your preferred style: How did it make you feel?

Eight of Swords (8)
Regeneration and new ways forward
on the psychological plane

Life lessons (imbalance/dis-ease): Fear of moving out of an oppressive situation; blocked by one's own thoughts; feeling trapped by equally frightening choices; waiting to be rescued.

Life wisdom (balanced energy/healing): Letting go of ideas and negative thought patterns that bind; liberation from an oppressive situation due to the courage to see things clearly and take appropriate action.

Actions to support the healing process: The Eight of Swords tells you that an answer will come—the problems to overcome or decisions to make will happen if you have a lion's heart and stay courageous. Take off the blindfold and see your situation clearly for the first time. You will not be paralyzed by your own fear forever if you drop "I can't" and "Yes, but" from your vocabulary. You have the power of choice and choice will liberate your healer within.

Examine your motives for staying in an oppressive relationship. Nothing prevents you from healing except negative thought patterns. A healing touch practitioner can help you open your chakras—pay special attention to the third, or solar plexus chakra: your sense of power and powerlessness; and the fifth, or throat chakra: the ability to speak up for yourself.

Contacting your inner wisdom: What am I avoiding? How can I take back my power?

Nine of Swords (9)

Completion on the psychological plane

Life lessons (imbalance/dis-ease): The "Nightmare Card"—unchecked fear and negative thought; fear of impending doom; paralyzed by guilt over the past, often with an unknown source; worry.

Life wisdom (balanced energy/healing): Liberation found in confronting one's own fears and pain; don't rush things; a little fear is a good thing, reasonable (healthy) fear helps us survive dangerous situations.

Actions to support the healing process: This card is about unchecked fear, self-doubt, or suspicion that results in physical illness and insomnia. The key to liberation (and completion of a cycle) is in taking action to confront the nightmare. Dream work will be especially beneficial in getting at the source of fear.

A trusted psychologist, counselor, or adviser is indicated to help you acknowledge your feelings of sadness, disillusion, and self-doubt. The unknown cause of your anguish is deep within your unconscious. Past-life readings or hypnosis can help you discover the source. Once the source of torment or shame is found, lasting change will be made.

Contacting your inner wisdom: How realistic are my fears? Am I willing to be patient enough to heal?

Ten of Swords (10)

Starting over at a higher cycle on the psychological plane

Life lessons (imbalance/dis-ease): Hysteria; hopelessness; being a victim (poor me); an inability to face pain; unable to let go.

Life wisdom (balanced energy/healing): A final, absolute letting go which allows for growth; coming to terms with what really is, not what one wanted or wished for.

Actions to support the healing process: There are no quick fixes—if you have had relief from physical ailments because of some external treatment, the Ten tells you to stay the course because lasting change comes from an absolute letting go of outworn habits and negative thought patterns.

If you "pick up the swords again" after your symptoms (and life) have calmed down, the situation will revert back to what it was. Also consider letting go of old methods of treatment that haven't been successful—try new ones until you find the treatment or intervention that's right for you.

This card is about the serenity to accept the things you cannot change, the courage to change the things you can, and the wisdom to know the difference.

Contacting your inner wisdom: What must I accept? What can I change? Do I know the difference between the two?

Wands: the spirit of illness and health in everyday actions

Suit of Tarot	Wands
Element	Fire
Level of illness or healing	Creativity, healing action, passion to change, anger, spirituality in everyday actions

Ace of Wands (1)

Beginnings, an upsurge of energy on the spiritual/creative plane

Life lessons (imbalance/dis-ease): Not trusting your own insight; not trusting your ability to heal; ignoring creative inspiration; too much undirected fiery energy.

Life wisdom (balanced energy/healing): A desire for growth and self-development; passion; inspiration; a spiritual search; rebirth of the Spirit.

Actions to support the healing process: It's time to move out of your stuck place. Your new direction will take you to a more creative and spiritual level of experience and understanding. You begin a new treatment or consult a new practitioner. The challenge of the Ace of Wands is staying focused and committed to the change in health habits.

You may find yourself being inspired by many approaches. You get all fired up about one, buy lots of expensive merchandise, only to lose interest and move on to the next inspiration. Ask yourself which endeavors should be tackled again and which ones discarded. As you awaken spiritually, your health will improve.

Your psychic explorations will make the mind-body connection a reality for you. You have the energy for creative endeavors, including pregnancy.

Contacting your inner wisdom: Do I act upon my inspirations? How is my self-image changing?

Two of Wands (2)

Balance or the need for balance on the spiritual/creative plane

Life lessons (imbalance/dis-ease): A feeling of restlessness; unexpressed creativity; dissatisfaction with life.

Life wisdom (balanced energy/healing): A wake-up call for action; the power of choice; change for the better is in the air; harnessing one's personal power to create.

Actions to support the healing process: If you have been stuck in an unhappy situation, don't be surprised if you decide to make changes all at once. Break out of your routine—take a different route to work, try something new, change your humdrum schedule.

While the Eight of Pentacles shows you busy working at something new, the Two of Wands provides the wakeup call you need to get started. This card urges you to do your homework and get busy making plans for change.

Stop procrastinating—make changes now. Because it is a Two, it asks you to find the balance in your life needed to complete your spiritual/creative tasks.

Contacting your inner wisdom: What creative inspiration do I need to act upon? In what ways do I honor the role of spirituality in my life?

Three of Wands (3)
Growth and expansion on the spiritual/creative plane

Life lessons (imbalance/dis-ease): Problems greater than expected; inability to grasp the higher overview (big picture); unwilling to try something new.

Life wisdom (balanced energy/healing): Initial completion of a project with the potential for expansion; new ideas forming on the horizon; a willingness to explore something new; creating your own future by visualizing it clearly.

Actions to support the healing process: The Three of Wands asks you to seek inner guidance on a daily basis, for there you will find your creative ideas. There is no difference between mind, body, and spirit—all reflect the same big picture. Study and practice techniques of creative visualization. Try *Practical Guide to Creative Visualization: Manifest Your Desires* by Denning and Phillips (Llewellyn, 2001).

Meditate with the Magician because he changes reality by visualizing goals, rolling up his sleeves and getting to work. With the energy of the Two of Wands behind you to balance work and play, you sense a shift within you at a very deep level.

You are learning that your outward creative projects are expressions of your inner, spiritual self. Your overall sense of well-being improves because of the actions you take to support the healing process.

Contacting your inner wisdom: Do I seek inner guidance on a daily basis? Can I see my life's purpose?

Four of Wands (4)

Stability or stagnation on the creative/spiritual plane

Life lessons (imbalance/dis-ease): Inability to appreciate success; lack of creative inspiration; failure to express joy.

Life wisdom (balanced energy/healing): Much-deserved rest after hard work; rite of passage; all is well, for now; harvest home; a time to pause and celebrate.

Actions to support the healing process: If you've been all work and no play, it's time to take a break and pat yourself on the back for all that you've accomplished. Your health and creativity suffer without the proper balance of work and play. Having a party or ritual with friends to honor a special occasion or event will renew your spirit.

You have laid a foundation of stability and healing through the choices you've made and actions you've taken. Celebrate the person you are becoming.

Contacting your inner wisdom: Do I create ways to celebrate the small victories in my life? What rite of passage do I need to honor and celebrate?

Five of Wands (5)
Conflict, struggle on the creative/spiritual plane

Life lessons (imbalance/dis-ease): Feeling the stress of petty obstacles; inner spiritual struggle; following a leader without thinking through our actions.

Life wisdom (balanced energy/healing): A sense of rules and fair play; the sharing of ideas in a creative group effort; the willingness to continue with plans and change course if necessary.

Actions to support the healing process: Energy needs to be used constructively or it is wasted and the moment is gone forever. Your health suffers if you spend time in petty conflicts, spinning your wheels, going nowhere, getting tired. If life seems to be moving too quickly, but going nowhere, you need a break. Slow down, quit fighting the small (but energy-draining) battles, pace yourself, and make time for your creative/spiritual activities.

   Seek support for your changing outlook on life from a like-minded group. The Five of Wands may indicate getting the runaround from groups—be assertive if your insurance company isn't playing fairly.

Contacting your inner wisdom: Can I let go of petty differences? Do I need to reorganize my priorities?

Six of Wands (6)

Harmony on the spiritual/creative plane

Life lessons (imbalance/dis-ease): Arrogance; looking for shortcuts to success or fame; faking it; insincerity; suspicion of other people's motives.

Life wisdom (balanced energy/healing): Leadership born of self-confidence; victory/success based on hard work; public recognition for a job well done.

Actions to support the healing process: You may find yourself on a spiritual quest to uncover hidden aspects of yourself. Make time for the workshop, retreat, seminar, or book that intrigues you. As you discover your spiritual/creative/psychic self, nagging physical complaints subside.

The more involved you are in your own healing process, the more energetic you feel. During daily meditation, you begin to receive the answers you need. Life starts to make sense. Don't be surprised if you find your life's calling, for the Six of Wands often means receiving spiritual gifts.

Contacting your inner wisdom: Can I recognize my own efforts and praise myself accordingly? Am I ready to move on to a new challenge?

Seven of Wands (7)

Inner work on the creative/spiritual plane

Life lessons (imbalance/dis-ease): Being defensive about actions or beliefs; fighting only for the adrenaline rush of being angry; not standing up for ourselves; fighting change.

Life wisdom (balanced energy/healing): Taking responsibility for our actions; enjoying competition because it is stimulating and exciting; acting from a position of strength.

Actions to support the healing process: Evaluate your present situation and your health. Do some soul-searching on how to prepare for change. People around you may become uncomfortable with your changes and try to put you on the defensive. Stand up for your newfound beliefs.

If you are resistant to changing behavior that is harmful to you, consider whether or not your attitudes come from a position of strength or defensiveness. If you need courage to change worn-out habits, take a tiny step toward a goal to help you feel more confident—gather information, make a call, ask questions, seek professional advice. Given time, your body's innate wisdom will rally to your defense.

Contacting your inner wisdom: Am I prepared to stand up for what I believe in? How does positive change and success affect me?

Eight of Wands (8)
Regeneration and new ways forward
on the creative/spiritual plane

Life lessons (imbalance/dis-ease): Ignoring an uncomfortable situation, hoping it will go away; procrastination; plunging into a situation before we are prepared.

Life wisdom (balanced energy/healing): A high-energy card directed toward a goal; a purposeful, productive period after a struggle; responding quickly when the time is right; realization of and using psychic energy to accomplish a goal.

Actions to support the healing process: You have an opportunity to take action on your own behalf. It may be tempting to seek quick fixes to physical ailments that have appeared suddenly. When your health is unsettled, it is natural to want things to improve quickly.

The Eight suggests sudden or impulsive action, but look closer at the picture. The Eight's true nature is *focused* energy going directly to its destination. This card reminds you to evaluate your health status or situation and *prioritize* before moving forward.

Discuss your plans with others and meditate for guidance from a higher source before you take action. Yes, it will look sudden to those around you, but change will come from a deep source of inner knowing.

Books about health and healing and workshops on alternative therapies will boost your immune system and speed up your healing process.

Contacting your inner wisdom: What are my goals and priorities? How can I focus my energy to achieve the best results?

Nine of Wands (9)

Completion on the creative/spiritual plane

Life lessons (imbalance/dis-ease): Exhaustion; tension; being at the end of your rope; immobilized by doubt.

Life wisdom (balanced energy/healing): Strength in reserve; the ability to go on no matter what life gives us; recognizing what must be healed.

Actions to support the healing process: You are willing to fight the good fight because you have chosen to face your problems and learn to cope with them. You have a willingness to know yourself more fully and you recognize what must be healed. Look to your past for unfinished business of an emotional or spiritual nature.

    Past-life readings and hypnosis can provide clues to your healing. Take the time to heal your wounds before making major plans/decisions about what to do next. You may feel like giving up—stay focused on all you've learned, your wisdom, because you're closer to wholeness than you think.

Contacting your inner wisdom: Do I make time for healing? What wisdom do I now have because of my life experiences?

Ten of Wands 10

Starting over at a higher cycle on the creative/spiritual plane

Life lessons (imbalance/dis-ease): Taking on too much, then being angry at self for doing it; overburdened with responsibilities; not being aware of personal limitations; unable to say no.

Life wisdom (balanced energy/healing): Being aware of personal limitations; carrying out responsibilities; not carrying the load for irresponsible people; saying no; setting limits; decreasing burdens to conserve energy.

Actions to support the healing process: You may be feeling tired, overworked, or just plain stressed out. Be honest with your loved ones and friends about what you can and cannot do. Set boundaries, limit time spent doing for others what they should be doing for themselves, delegate responsibility, resign from that volunteer officer position, stop being superwoman.

Spend time alone doing anything that calms and centers you. Finish that creative project—the one that gives you joy but you never have time for anymore. Speak up, tell people what you need from them and nurture your creative healer within.

Contacting your inner wisdom: Do I let my responsibilities overshadow the joy of living? Do I prevent others from developing important skills by assuming their responsibility?

Section C: Court Cards

The people, personalities, and healers of tarot

No other cards in the tarot deck have more interpretations. Read any tarot book and you'll find different meanings and names. These sixteen cards can be challenging because you have to decide if they represent another person or some aspect of yourself—or both. I'll make it simple. The Court Cards *are always a reflection of you:* you draw the people to you that *you* need for *your* life lesson/ life wisdom. So, it doesn't matter if it describes someone else—the card is still about *you* and *your* need to have those qualities in your life.

We all have qualities that are traditionally associated with masculine and feminine ways of being. For instance, a woman can be competitive and a man can be nurturing. Be aware that the King and Knight can represent a woman and the Queen can symbolize a man. The gender or "occupation" of the court card is less important than the qualities it describes.

Pages can represent a child, but they also introduce the element of their suit, the willingness to change or learn something new. Pages also carry messages related to their suit. *Knights* represent young adults or someone starting over, focusing on a specific task. Because they focus on the task at hand, Knights signify the need for a therapist based on the energy of their suit.

Queens are mature. They take their understanding of life inward and use this life wisdom to nurture others and encourage self-development. Because they are the embodiment of the feminine tradition of healing, Queens represent the need for a healer in relationship to their suit. *Kings* are also mature, but they project their maturity outward in the form of leadership. They take charge and give advice specific to their suit. In a healing layout, the King indicates the need for a physician/adviser.

Most traditional tarot books start with the suit of Wands, representing the creative fire, and end with Pentacles, symbolizing the stability of earth. I reverse the order of suits because I follow the alignment of our chakras, or energy centers along our spine. We start with the *body* (Pentacles) and work our way through *emotions* (Cups), *psychological makeup* (Swords), and *spirit* (Wands). This corresponds to the four levels of illness and health described throughout the book.

Pentacle Court Cards
The physical plane of illness and health

Page of Pentacles
Messages from the physical plane of illness and health

Life lessons (imbalance/dis-ease): Living a life of excess without having a sense of what is truly valuable; low self-esteem; unwillingness to prepare; holding onto unrealistic goals; being illogical and impatient, ignoring or not trusting instincts.

Life wisdom (balanced energy/healing): Beginning awareness of the need to be slow and patient; being open to learning and preparation; building realistic goals slowly, from the ground up; trusting instincts; gaining experience.

Actions to support the healing process: The Page of Pentacles message is from the body and instinctual nature. Listen to what your body is trying to tell you because your instincts are correct: if you're hungry, eat. If you're tired, rest.

People with stress-related illness often get this card. Any physical problem you are having may be your inner self trying to get your attention. Realize you may be in for the long haul and prepare to see things through. You have had it with treatments that don't work—try something new.

Contacting your inner wisdom: Am I willing to make a commitment to my healing? What are my instincts trying to tell me?

Knight of Pentacles
Therapist/Counselor

Life lessons (imbalance/dis-ease): Being overly cautious or dogged; laziness; lack of discipline; inability to make plans and carry them out; irresponsibility; lack of imagination; impractical.

Life wisdom (balanced energy/healing): Determination; practicality; being completely reliable; perseverance; being able to focus on the important issues; focusing on the body, work, money, or anything that is considered valuable.

Actions to support the healing process: Prioritize your health care—what is most important to you? Focus on your body or any work/money issue that is stressing you. A therapist or counselor will be helpful in sorting out what you value. Focus on health habits that may be harming your body, especially those with long-term consequences.

Contacting your inner wisdom: What do I most value? Do I have a plan for healing?

Queen of Pentacles
Healer

Life lessons (imbalance/dis-ease): Stubbornness; the need to control; being overly concerned with work or money; finding no value or satisfaction in work; not being able to help or nurture others; hating the body; having an unhealthy relationship with food.

Life wisdom (balanced energy/healing): Love of body; generous and nurturing; in tune with nature and the cycles of life; flexible; allowing others to find their own way; having a healthy relationship with food.

Actions to support the healing process: If you could be pregnant, get a test now. Evaluate your relationship with food: is it excessive or anorexic? Keep a food journal for a week and record everything that you eat, right down to the fuzzy Lifesaver in the bottom of your pocket. Include the place you eat and how you are feeling at the time. Look at the record for gaps in nutrition and possible emotional eating. Get help if you have an eating disorder.

Bodywork such as massage will greatly help you get in touch with your physical self; so will a healer who specializes in physical problems. Healing touch will be beneficial. Aromatherapy will appeal to your senses. Look for ways to nurture yourself and others on a regular basis.

Contacting your inner wisdom: Am I able to nurture myself? What are my attitudes toward pleasure and sensuality? What is my relationship with food?

King of Pentacles
Physician/Adviser

Life lessons (imbalance/dis-ease): Being status-conscious and materialistic; distrusting spirituality; greed; slow to change; having a mean streak; being completely out of touch with the body or overly concerned with it—vanity; workaholic.

Life wisdom (balanced energy/healing): Finding a balance between work and play; being solid, steady, and practical; disciplined; having ambition based on an inner sense of values; being content with what you have; success through hard work.

Actions to support the healing process: Remember that all work and no play make Jack a dull boy. If money worries are making you sick, seek the aid of a financial adviser. Tension may show up in your neck, shoulders, and knees. In this case, the King represents the need for an orthopedic physician, chiropractor, or any other specialist to help you with muscular pain. If you feel restless and don't know why, seek spiritual answers with the same energy you apply to work and making money.

Contacting your inner wisdom: What value do I place in money, work, career, and financial security? Do I need to play more and work less?

Cup Court Cards
The emotional plane of illness and health

Page of Cups
Messages from the emotional plane of illness and health

Life lessons (imbalance/dis-ease): Unwillingness to be open to emotional change; emotionally immature; restlessness; running away from any uncomfortable emotions; fantasizing.

Life wisdom (balanced energy/healing): Listening to the heart; the opening of the inner voice; willingness to take an emotional risk because of love; being open to the development and maturation of feelings.

Actions to support the healing process: Your negative emotions show up in your body as physical ailments. It is tempting to look for emotional "quick fixes" like overeating, or use of tranquilizers and alcohol. Instead of drowning your emotions in external substances, first pay attention to the messages from your emotions: don't ignore any negative emotion and its message to change your outlook.

Contacting your inner wisdom: Am I willing to explore my emotional nature? What is the message from my emotions or dreams?

Knight of Cups
Therapist/Counselor

Life lessons (imbalance/dis-ease): Self-absorption; withdrawal from reality to focus on fantasy and daydreams; acting out of emotions; emotional manipulation of others; playboy or playgirl; superficial.

Life wisdom (balanced energy/healing): Striving for emotional balance; focusing on emotions; the ability to make friends; falling in love; focusing on dream work and having healing dreams; defending your ideals.

Actions to support the healing process: Seek the assistance of a counselor or therapist to help you focus on troubling emotions and sort them out. Volunteer for a cause you believe in and really "put your heart into it"— your ideals need expression.

Find constructive ways to express your powerful emotions: exercise, dance, learn a martial art, take up painting, learn to play a musical instrument, visit an art museum, anything that will allow you to focus your emotional energies in a positive way. You will also benefit from physical activities involving water. Keep a dream journal. Ask for and expect a healing dream. Focus on emotional development in all relationships.

Contacting your inner wisdom: What are my ideals? What are my dreams? How can I establish emotional boundaries in my relationships?

Queen of Cups
Healer

Life lessons (imbalance/dis-ease): So immersed in the inner world, the outer world of everyday life may be baffling; emotional possessiveness and jealousy; unfaithfulness in love relationships; unable to tolerate the emotional pain of others; denying psychic ability.

Life wisdom (balanced energy/healing): Emotional understanding that nurtures others; sensitivity to emotional pain; loyalty in friendships and love—relationships; having psychic skills and understanding they are gifts; emotional maturity.

Actions to support the healing process: The Queen represents emotional healing. Seek the assistance of a healer who understands the importance of—and is willing to work with—the emotional level of illness and healing. Consult a psychic, get a past-life reading to help you understand how past emotional issues are affecting you now.

Develop your own psychic ability because the time is right for discovery of the inner world. Your emotions have a powerful impact on your health: seek alternative forms of treatment if traditional methods have not given you emotional satisfaction. Share your emotional wisdom with others, for you have much to offer.

Contacting your inner wisdom: Do I trust my feelings? Do I trust my psychic ability?

King of Cups
Physician/Adviser

Life lessons (imbalance/dis-ease): Emotional mistrust; jealousy to the point of rage; hedonism; emotional dishonesty; self-importance; intolerance; emotional weakness.

Life wisdom (balanced energy/healing): Feelings under control with a detached awareness; being effective in emotional crises; the wounded healer (healing self by healing others); seeing the humor in emotionally charged situations.

Actions to support the healing process: Seek an emotional adviser—someone who has been there. If you have a problem with alcohol or drugs, attend twelve-step meetings and find your King of Cups in the form of a sponsor. The King can also represent the need for a psychiatrist—literally, a physician who gives emotional advice.

Give of yourself to others—like the Queen, you have much to share. Watch for excessive appetites of any kind. Swimming, sailing, trips to the beach, or a picnic by a lake will all help calm the turbulent waters of your emotions. Ride the wave of your fluctuating moods, because they will pass.

Contacting your inner wisdom: Do I participate in my own healing process before I attempt to heal others? What emotional wisdom do I have to share?

Sword Court Cards
The psychological level of illness and healing

Page of Swords
Messages from the psychological plane of illness and health

Life lessons (imbalance/dis-ease): Inaction due to fear or depression; a whirlwind of thought that goes nowhere; making decisions without regard to logic or reason; unwilling to make a decision that involves risk.

Life wisdom (balanced energy/healing): Facing fears and depression head-on; being open to intellectual development, study, and learning; developing a deeper understanding of self and personal philosophies.

Actions to support the healing process: Seek legal, medical, or surgical assistance. The message of the Page is through communication and the written word. Pay attention to warning signs of illness (symptoms that won't go away, abnormal laboratory tests or biopsies, diagnostics of any type), for they carry important information about your dis-ease.

Lingering health problems demand that you research the facts so you can come up with a treatment plan that suits your needs. You may be spending long hours in the library to get the information you need. In a layout of many Swords, especially the Three of Swords, surgery may be indicated.

Contacting your inner wisdom: Do I need to cut myself off from a painful past? Do I need more information before I can make a decision? What is my personal philosophy of life?

Knight of Swords
Therapist/Counselor

Life lessons (imbalance/dis-ease): Starting projects with excitement and ending abruptly in chaos; being too impatient to wait for anything; cold logic without feeling;

Life wisdom (balanced energy/healing): Focusing on thoughts, beliefs, and philosophies; focusing on a decision that needs to be made; being versatile and adaptable to change.

Actions to support the healing process: The Knight indicates the need for a therapist/counselor who will focus on thinking patterns and beliefs that inhibit the healing process—stuck ways of thinking that are holding you back.

    If you are into a life of busyness, this card means you need to slow down and examine what you are avoiding by keeping so busy. Focus on control of your own treatment decisions. Use your research skills to arrive at a solution that is right for you. Meditation will help you focus your thoughts, so you can listen to your heart and not your head.

Contacting your inner wisdom: Do I need to slow down? Where do I need to focus my thoughts?

Queen of Swords
Healer

Life lessons (imbalance/dis-ease): Cold and aloof; unforgiving; rigidity of viewpoint; ultracritical; failing to balance emotions and rational thought.

Life wisdom (balanced energy/healing): The one who lives, loves, and loses—and lives to love again. Commonly refers to a widow; spiritual depth caused by prolonged struggle; tolerant and easygoing; political consciousness.

Actions to support the healing process: You may need to see a grief counselor or a healer specializing in sorrow and loss. Take a timeout from painful emotions in favor of introspection. Keeping a journal will appeal to the Queen of the written word.

Writing of any type will help you understand the way your mind works. You are literally taking your pain unto yourself. Look deeply at your physical symptoms—they are an expression of negative thought patterns and worn-out beliefs that are making you ill. Reevaluate your ideals.

Contacting your inner wisdom: What intellectual abilities do I need to nurture? What has my sorrow taught me? How can my life experience be of benefit to others?

King of Swords
Physician/Adviser

Life lessons (imbalance/dis-ease): Ruthless quest for power; selfishness; using the intellect to dominate others; pride, arrogance; corrupted authority.

Life wisdom (balanced energy/healing): Authority earned through disciplined mental effort; good judgment; lover of truth and justice; fairness above all; diplomatic.

Actions to support the healing process: If you have been thinking of taking up a cause, especially in the health arena, do so, but your power is in the written word, not force. Say what you think and feel, for you offer great truths.

You have an inner knowing that will force you out into the world to act upon it. You must speak your mind to stay healthy. If work is making you ill, the King will give you the power to negotiate a better situation.

If you are having difficulty with a painful past or negative thought patterns, seek the help of a psychologist. The King can represent a surgeon. If a battery of tests indicate surgery, do some research of your own to educate yourself on the topic. Become an informed consumer.

This King, above all, takes responsibility for his health care choices and makes decisions based on facts. You may also find yourself having an intellectual curiosity about all things esoteric: read, study, and research.

Contacting your inner wisdom: Do I speak my truths? Can I allow others to speak theirs? Does pride ever get in my way?

Wand Court Cards
The creative/spiritual level of illness
and healing in everyday actions

Page of Wands
Messages from the creative/spiritual plane of illness and health

Life lessons (imbalance/dis-ease): Acting impulsively; refusing to take risks of any kind; being unpredictable; fiery temper; having a feeling of burnout.

Life wisdom (balanced energy/healing): Active imagination; willing to take a creative risk; being on fire with creative passion; having a strong (and healthy) sex drive; being inspired.

Actions to support the healing process: The Page carries the message of creative inspiration. Since computers have crystals in them, your message of creative inspiration may be computer-related or come from the Internet. Telephone calls may also bring significant messages.

Look for opportunities to develop your creative talents through career, hobby, or study. Listen to inspirational speakers, read inspirational books. Without creative activities/outlets in your life, you will be prone to depression and illness. To stay well, you must do what inspires you and follow your bliss. Routine depresses you, but you need a little routine to balance all the creative energy.

Since you have a tendency to burn the candle at both ends, changes in your lifestyle will greatly improve health: get enough rest, eat right, exercise, meditate—your fiery energy will be renewed. Concentrate on one day at a time.

Contacting your inner wisdom: What inspires me? What new direction do I need to take?

Knight of Wands
Therapist/counselor

Life lessons (imbalance/dis-ease): Taking life too seriously; depression; boredom; lack of discipline to pursue goals; irresponsible behavior; being scattered.

Life wisdom (balanced energy/healing): Easy creativity; focused on creative and inspirational pursuits; focused on spirituality; playful; the spirit of adventure.

Actions to support the healing process: When the Knight appears, your focus is on all things creative, for it is the creative act that gives you a connection to something greater than yourself—your creative activities are an expression of your spirituality in everyday actions.

If you need help finding a spiritual (creative) focus, seek the assistance of a counselor or therapist specializing in spiritual guidance, for it is here you will find your meaning in life. Seek new challenges. One of your challenges is to determine if your energy overwhelms others—setting limits with yourself will help you find balance.

For nagging health problems to get better, you need to identify work that will inspire you (boredom causes depression) and then create a plan to help you achieve your goals. Meditate with the Magician—the two of you have a lot in common.

Contacting your inner wisdom: Do I put my spirituality into action in the everyday world? On what creative endeavor do I need to focus?

Queen of Wands
Healer

Life lessons (imbalance/dis-ease): Extravagance; pride; vanity; temper; having little insight into spirituality; lack of confidence; self-righteousness; feeling overwhelmed.

Life wisdom (balanced energy/healing): Loyalty; understanding spirituality and the need to be creative; the modern woman: able to juggle career, family, and social obligations at one time; nurturing others and encouraging spiritual growth; intuitive.

Actions to support the healing process: If you are struggling with the obligations of life, slow down, take the time to rest. Learn to say no to avoid feeling scattered. Enjoy the journey. If you feel nervous, explore an herb and health food store for the right treatment. Ask an expert and use caution, but a fiery herb such as ginseng may give you the energy boost you need.

For spiritual and creative concerns, seek the assistance of a healer who understands the energetics of healing and can work with chakra balancing. A healing touch treatment will balance your energy on all levels and help you with anger management. Share your spiritual views with others for you have much wisdom.

Contacting your inner wisdom: Do I follow my hunches? Do I take the time to be creative? How can I take charge of my own life?

King of Wands
Physician/Adviser

Life lessons (imbalance/dis-ease): Domineering; hot-tempered; impulsive; con man; having selfish motives; bigoted; histrionic.

Life wisdom (balanced energy/healing): Making decisions based on intuitive flashes of insight; optimistic with a strong sense of self; able to forgive others; having a strong personal spirituality.

Actions to support the healing process: Of all the Court Cards, the King of Wands is the "Type A" personality and has the biggest problem with anger management. Anger affects your health on all levels: migraines, high blood pressure, ulcers, heartburn. The King also represents the physician/adviser. Seek assistance from a physician who can help you with anger management (a psychiatrist) or a doctor who can help you with your anger-related symptoms, such as an internist.

Experiment with new treatments until you find what works for you. Pinpoint what angers you and take steps to rectify it before you literally blow a fuse. Spiritual concerns are best addressed with the guidance of a spiritual adviser. Consider being a mentor or spiritual adviser yourself and share those laser-like insights. You have many wonderful ideas: your talents are best used in situations where you are the ideas person, the creative spark to get things going. Be realistic—routine and small details make you angry and cause dis-ease. Avoid jobs that lack imagination.

Contacting your inner wisdom: Do I acknowledge and use my leadership abilities? Do I allow my creativity to flow unrestricted?

Bibliography

Akner, Lois F., C.S.W. *How to Survive the Loss of a Parent: A Guide for Adults.* New York: Quill, William Morrow, 1993.

Arrien, Angeles. *The Four-Fold Way.* San Francisco: HarperSanFrancisco, 1993.

Arroyo, Stephen. M.A. *Astrology, Psychology and the Four Elements: An Energy Approach to Astrology and Its Use in the Counseling Arts.* Sebastopol, Calif.: CRCS Publications, 1975.

Avery, Brice. *Principles of Psychotherapy.* San Francisco: Thornsons, An Imprint of HarperCollins Publishers, 1996.

Bowes, Susan. *Life Magic.* New York: Simon and Schuster, 1999.

Bradford, Michael. *The Healing Energy of Your Hands.* Freedom, Calif.: The Crossing Press, 1993.

Brennan, Barbara Ann. *Hands of Light: A Guide to Healing Through the Human Energy Field.* New York: Bantam Books, 1987.

————. *Light Emerging: The Journal of Personal Healing.* 1993.

Campbell, Eileen, and J. H. Brennan. *Body, Mind and Spirit: A Dictionary of New Age Ideas, People, Places and Terms.* Boston: Charles E. Tuttle Company, Inc., 1994.

Cameron, Julia. *The Artist's Way: A Spiritual Path to Higher Creativity.* New York: Penguin Putnam, 1992.

Choquette, Sonia. *The Psychic Pathway: A Workbook for Reawakening the Voice of Your Soul.* New York: Crown Trade Paperbacks, 1995.

Friedlander, John and Gloria Hemsher. *Basic Psychic Development: A User's Guide to Auras, Chakras and Clairvoyance.* York Beach, Maine: Samuel Weiser, Inc. 1999.

Giles, Cynthia. *The Tarot: History, Mystery and Lore.* New York: A Fireside Book by Simon and Schuster, 1992.

————. *The Tarot: Methods, Mastery and More.* 1996.

Greer, Mary K. *Tarot for Your Self.* North Hollywood, Calif.: Newcastle Publishing Co., 1884.

Gwain, Rose. *Discovering Yourself Through the Tarot: A Jungian Guide to Archetypes and Personality.* Rochester, Vir.: Destiny Books, 1994.

Harvey, A. McGehee, M.D., et. al., *The Principles and Practice of Medicine.* New York: Appleton-Century-Crofts, 1980.

Hay, Louise L. *Heal Your Body.* Carlsbad, Calif.: Hay House, Inc., 1982.

Hooper, E. *The River: A Journey to the Source of HIV and AIDS.* Boston: Little Brown and Company, 1999.

Hover-Kramer, Dorthea, Ed.D., R.N. *Healing Touch: A Resource for Health Care Professionals.* Boston: Delmar Publishers, 1996.

Irving, Washington. *The Sketch Book,* "The Legend of Sleepy Hollow (first published in 1820), New York: Signet Classic, Penguin Books, USA, Inc., 1981.

Johnson, Cait and Maura D. Shaw. *Tarot Games: 45 Playful Ways to Explore Tarot Cards Together.* San Francisco: HarperSanFrancisco, 1994.

Jette, Christine. *Tarot Shadow Work.* St. Paul: Llewellyn Publications, 2000.

Keegan, Lynn, Ph.D., R.N. *The Nurse as Healer.* Albany: Delmar Publishers, Inc., 1994.

Kennedy, Alexandra. *Losing a Parent: Passage to a New Way of Living.* New York: HarperCollins, 1991.

Kennedy, David Daniel. *Feng Shui: Tips for a Better Life.* Pownal, Ver.: Storey Books, 1998.

Kopp, Sheldon. *Raise Your Right Hand Against Fear: Extend the Other in Compassion.* New York: Ballantine Books, 1988.

Krieger, Dolores. *Accepting Your Power to Heal: The Personal Practice of Therapeutic Touch.* Santa Fe: Bear and Company, 1993.

Kunz, Dora, editor. *Spiritual Aspects of the Healing Arts.* Wheaton, Ill.: The Theosophical Publishing House, 1985.

————. *Spiritual Healing.* 1995.

Lloyd, Carol. *Creating a Life Worth Living.* New York: HarperCollins, 1997.

MacGregor, Trish and Phyllis Vega. *Power Tarot.* New York: Fireside Books, 1998.

Metzger, Deena. *Writing for Your Life: A Guide and Companion to the Inner Worlds.* San Francisco: HarperSanFrancisco, 1992.

Mosby's Conventional Medicine/Alternative Medicine: Choices of Treatment for Your Most Common Medical Problems. Caroline Green, editor. St. Louis: Mosby-Year Books, Inc., 1998.

Mosby's Pocket Dictionary of Medicine, Nursing and Allied Health. Kenneth N. Anderson, editor. St. Louis: The C. V. Mosby Company, 1990.

Noble, Vicki. *Making Ritual with Motherpeace Cards.* New York: Three Rivers Press, 1998.

Pollack, Rachel. *Seventy-Eight Degrees of Wisdom: A Book of Tarot.* San Francisco: Thorsons, HarperCollins, 1997.

Renée, Janina. *Tarot Spells.* St. Paul: Llewellyn Publications, 1995.

Roach, Sally, MSN, R.N. and Beatriz Nieto, MSN, R.N. *Healing and the Grief Process.* Albany: Delmar Publishers, Inc., 1997.

Schermer, Barbara. *Astrology Alive: A Guide to Experiential Astrology and the Healing Arts.* Freedom, Calif.: The Crossing Press, 1998.

Shore, Lesley Irene, Ph.D. *Healing the Feminine: Reclaiming Women's Voice.* St. Paul: Llewellyn Publications, 1995.

Sontag, Susan. *Illness as Metaphor and AIDS and Its Metaphors.* New York: Anchor Books Doubleday, 1989.

Stein, Diane. *The Women's Book of Healing.* St. Paul: Llewellyn Publications, 1994.

Streep, Peg. *Altars Made Easy: A Guide to Creating Your Own Personal Space.* New York: HarperCollins, 1997.

Taber's Cyclopedic Medical Dictionary. Clayton L. Thomas, M.D., editor. Philadelphia: F. A. Davis Company, 1993.

Tierra, Michael and Candis Cantin. *The Spirit of Herbs: A Guide to the Herbal Tarot.* Stamford, Conn.: U.S. Games, Inc., 1993.

Weed, Susun. *Menopausal Years The Wise Woman Way.* Woodstock, New York: Ash Tree Publishing, 1992.

Index

A

activities that support the healing process, 6, 90

affirmations, see *intention to heal*

altar, as healing sanctuary, 11–12, 23, 35, 43, 53–54, 58, 62, 69–70, 73, 76, 93, 105, 151

alternative therapies, 143, 186

anger, as cause of dis-ease (also see *headless horsemen*), 21, 42–43, 47–50, 55, 60, 78, 108, 112–113, 168, 173, 179, 204–205

attitudes, role of in healing, 3, 67, 120, 141, 149, 152, 185, 192

awakening the healer within, also see *creative healer*, 46, 125, 188

activities using tarot, see table of contents

B

balance, see *homeostasis, karma*

breaking the pain cycle, 5, 104

going within to stop pain, 104, 106

breathing deeply, 58, 73, 82

method of meditation, 58, 73

prerequisite to tarot work, 58, 73, 82

busyness, impediment to healing, 68, 77, 91, 199

C

centering, 5, 18–19, 22, 77, 90–91, 93, 165–166

choice, power of, 173, 176, 180

conscious mind and unconscious body, 50–52

need for counseling, 60

creating sacred space, altar, 6, 11–12, 23, 35, 43, 53–54, 58, 62, 69–70, 73, 76, 93, 105, 151

creative healer, 46, 125, 188

creative visualization, 167, 181

creativity, blocked,
and healing, 39
and illness, 39

crone, see *wisewoman healer and witch*

curing vs. healing, 87–88, 90

W

CPSIA information can be obtained at www.ICGtesting.com
Printed in the USA
LVOW111649220413

330337LV00010B/402/P

9 780738 700434